Air Fryer Cookbook for Beginners

Make The Most Of Your Air Fryer

And Simple&Fabulous Recipes

Winona D. Reaves

Table of Contents

There are two possible reasons you've picked up this air fryer cookbook: you're thinking of buying this counter workhorse, and you're not sure whether you should buy one or you're ready to purchase the next best kitchen gadget.

Well, I've got good news! Even with all the clutter in your kitchen, an air fryer is something you'll clear some room for, especially if you're a cooking enthusiast. As someone who loves taking the time to try new healthy, and mouthwatering dishes, I understand how tempting it is to look at a new cooking tech and resist buying it immediately.

Unfortunately, your counter space is a hot commodity, and the last thing you need is a bulky kitchen appliance- one that you don't know how to use- taking up space. Before making a new purchase, you need to learn what an air fryer is, its pros and cons, how you can use it, and how to maintain it.

What if I told you that's precisely what I'll teach you in this fantastic cookbook? In this comprehensive guide to air fryers, I'll help you learn the basics of this innovative kitchen appliance and how it's different from a deep fryer. After that, you can use this handy gadget to try air fryer recipes you've saved on your Insta for the past couple of months. And here's the best part: you can use this kitchen appliance to make almost everything, including your favorite appetizers, main dishes, and desserts.

Next, we'll jump onto the endless benefits of purchasing and using an air fryer. Here you'll discover how to cook your favorite, healthy dishes without all the oil, mess, and unnecessary cleanup. You'll also learn *why* everyone is crazy about the air fryer and its quick and easy-to-use features.

Finally, after discussing whether air fryers are as healthy as everyone, I'll teach you my secret tips for keeping your air fryer clean, your kitchen spotless, and your fingers intact. As a newbie to the kitchen gadget world, I also struggled to understand what was perfect for my desired dish and when and how I needed to detach my air fryer. So, I'll save you the trouble of pulling at the gadget for five minutes before realizing you have clicked the button by going over some newbie mistakes to avoid.

Ready to make your final decision? With my in-depth air fryer cookbook, you can rest assured you'll have all the info necessary to make an informed decision:

An Introduction to Air Fryers

To join the air fryer club, you must first learn this kitchen gadget's basics. In this chapter, I'll help you answer questions like 'what are air fryers' and 'how do they work.'

A Quick Glance at Air Fryers

Air fryers are miniature, easy-to-use convection oven that fits perfectly on your kitchen countertop. The kitchen appliance claims to mimic deep-fryers with only hot air and little to no oil.

The gadget has been gaining popularity since 2020, especially since it will cook most anything! From crispy fries and wings to a yummy pizza, air fryers allow you to cook foods you could deep fry or make in the oven but with very little oil.

Air Fryers vs.Deep Fryers

Often confused with each other, air fryers and deep fryers allow you to cook similar foods but have several apparent differences. While air fryers use a high-powered fan for baking food at high temperatures, deep fryers cook food in oil heated to the desired temperature.

Both kitchen gadgets help you cook yummy dishes quickly, but air fryers don't require preheating time, whereas deep fryers take 5 to 10 minutes. Furthermore, foods cooked in air fryers require very little oil and deep requires significant amounts.

Lastly, you can enjoy cooking crispy and juicy foods with both appliances, but they won't always taste the same. Why? Because you need to spray battered foods with oil before placing them in your air fryer to get the crispy, tantalizing flavour your taste buds crave. However, since the hot oil soaks into the batter in deep-fryers, flour-based batters don't cook well in air fryers.

Air Fryers vs. Ovens

In many ways, air fryers are fan ovens. However, certain qualities make this kitchen appliance stand out.

Firstly, since air fryers are countertop kitchen gadgets, they're more compact and lightweight than an oven. Its smaller capacity mixed with a high-powered fan and power source means this appliance cooks your favorite meals faster.

In addition, unlike ovens, air fryers don't require preheating time, meaning you can speed up meal prep and cook dishes in half the time.

How Does an Air Fryer Work?

Air fryers use convection heat to help you cook healthy and delicious foods. The device comprises a fan that circulates hot air above and around your food to convert moisture into mist.

Once you place your food inside the appliance, the extra-hot chamber relies on the Maillard reaction. As a result, the food gets penetrated from the inside out, with a crispy exterior and tender insides.

A bonus point of air fryers is that it saves you time and reduces messes.

Step-by-Step Guide to Using an Air Fryer

Start making tasty dishes in your air fryer by learning how to use it:

Step # 1: Placing Food in the Basket

The air fryer basket can typically hold between 2 to 10 quarts to help make delicious dishes. I recommend adding one to two tablespoons of oil to make crispy and tasty dishes.

But if you're short on time, you can put a foil in this gadget to avoid unnecessary messes.

Step # 2: Setting Time and Temperature

The real air frying challenge: setting the air fryer at the perfect time and temperature.

Depending on the dish you're trying, air fryer cooking times and temperatures may vary between 5 and 25 minutes and 350 o and 400oF.

Step # 3: Waiting for the Magic to Happen

Relax as the air fryer cooks flavorful dishes half the time. Sometimes, you might flip or turn the food halfway to ensure the final version is evenly crispy and well-cooked.

What Delicious Things Can You Cook in an Air Fryer?

If there's one thing air fryers are best at, it's cooking crispy and delicious food, locked with nutrients and flavor. But if you're a newbie trying an air fryer for the first time, you're likely struggling to understand what you can cook in the air fryer.

Here's the good news: you can use air fryers to create diverse meals. No, you don't need to stick with deep-friend recipes; you can also use this innovative kitchen gadget to:

Fry Yummylicious Frozen Finger Foods

Air fryers are perfect for preparing frozen foods, including French fries, mozzarella sticks, and chicken nuggets. Skip your deep fryer and try making frozen air-fried foods to lower oil usage and make your taste buds dance.

Re-create Appetizing Finger Foods

If you're a fan of making homemade finger foods, the air fryer is a fantastic tool for making crispy and tender snacks and appetizers.

Try cooking sweet potato fries, potato chips, pickles, and egg rollers from scratch in an air fryer. It uses less oil but maintains the taste and crispiness of the snack.

Cook Chicken, Fish, and Meat to Enjoy a Healthy Meal

The pro of using air fryers for cooking chicken, fish, and meat is that it'll be tender, juicy, and healthy. Try air-fryer chicken recipes like keto meatballs, air fryer chicken and vegetables, and air fryer chicken tenders to satisfy your love for delicious foods.

If you're a fan of seafood, you can try air fryer cod, air fryer fish with garlic and lemon, air fryer crumb-topped sole, or air fryer fish and chips.

You can try air fryer steak bites and mushrooms if you want to dig in a delicious meat steak. You can also make juicy steak bites or air fryer roast beef.

Roasting Vegetables

Air fryers are also perfect for roasting vegetables, especially if you cook for two people. Enjoy a healthy and delicious dinner by trying air fryer herb and lemon cauliflower, air fryer asparagus, or garlic-rosemary brussels sprouts.

The Benefits of Air Fryers- Why Do I Need One?

Air fryers cook foods by convection which helps create crispy and tender food with minimal fat. Thus, air-fried food is a lot healthier than deep-fried foods. But that's not the only benefit air fryers offer.

Here are several reasons I recommend choosing an air fryer:

Low Cost

One thing I'm sure you'll appreciate about an air fryer is that it helps you save costs. Quality cooking oil can be expensive, mainly if you're using a lot. And when using deep fryers, you'll have to add plenty of oil.

Since air fryers use minimum oil, you don't have to spend a lot of cash buying cooking oil. Moreover, you can use the same cooking oil a couple of times before it gets dirty and you have to throw it away.

In addition, air fryers use comparatively less energy than ovens. Thus, it helps you save electricity and helps lower your utility bills.

Low-Fat Meals

Air fryers use comparatively less oil. In fact, an in-depth study by NIH confirmed that air-fried food is substantially lower in fat than deep-fried.

Air fryers achieve this by circulating hot air, which contains oil droplets. In that way, switching to air-fried foods can aid in losing weight.

Thus, air fryers are better for people who want to eat healthier and shed kilos.

Easy to Clean

No one enjoys figuring out how an appliance works and using it forever. Air fryers make this task easier with their straightforward controls.

The best part is that each part of the air fryer is removable. As a result, you can disassemble it for thorough cleaning and washing. And here's a bonus: you can wash it in your dishwasher!

It gets better. Since you're the minimal amount of oil, you won't have to spend hours scrubbing the appliance. Mix soap and warm water to get your air fryer looking as good as new.

Crunchy Texture

Does this sound like: you love the taste of fried, crunchy food but don't want a lot of fat? Then air fryers are the perfect option for you.

Its high-powered fan helps you cook crispy and crunchy food with fewer calories. And here's a secret tip: flip your food halfway through the cooking process to get an evenly crunchy exterior and tender interior.

Avoid Acrylamide Formation

Here's something you probably don't know: frying food in oil can lead to the development of acrylamide.

According to research, this dangerous compound can develop breast, endometrial, esophageal, and pancreatic cancer. Furthermore, studies also suggest a link between acrylamide and kidney and ovarian cancer.Using air fryers can lower your use of oil, thus decreasing the risk of acrylamide and subsequent illnesses.

More Efficient than Oven Cooking

One thing I love about air fryers- and I'm sure you will too- is that it gets hot quickly. In addition, the powerful fan circulating air helps ensure your food stays evenly browned and crispy. Thus, you can cut your cooking time efficiently.

But that's not the only reason cooking in an air fryer is more efficient! The size of the air fryer compared to your oven saves you the trouble of heating the oven beforehand. Therefore, you can put your food in the air fryer basket, slide it in, set the time, and get a delicious meal within ten to twenty minutes. So, air fryers are perfect for quick, easy snacks for a party or after-school treat.

Air Fryer Use and Maintenance

Air fryers are an excellent investment. It has become the most commonly used frying device in households. With its unique properties of minimal to no oil to fry different food items, people have become more interested in the appliance.

Air fryers are versatile as you can cook meals like fish, chicken, or meat, side dishes, healthy vegetables, appetizers such as chicken wings and zucchini fries, or even delicious desserts. Air fryers are perfect for cooking food items that you want extra crunchy such as fried chicken, French fries, potato wedges, or even baked potato with skin. It is a perfect kitchen appliance for cooking meats such as chicken or steak since they will always turn juicy and succulent.

However, to enjoy mouthwatering meals, it is crucial to maintain the appliance to ensure it functions perfectly. Apart from regular cleaning, air fryers need essential maintenance to ensure it does not get damaged. The maintenance includes:

- Checking cords before using the appliance. Ensure you do not plug a damaged or frayed cord into the electric socket. It can lead to serious injury. Also, it is crucial to ensure the cords are clean and damage-free before plugging them into the outlet.
- It is crucial to ensure the appliance is clean and free of any leftover debris from meals cooked earlier. If you haven't used your air fryer for a long time, inspect the insides thoroughly before you prepare meals. Clean it gently and remove any dirt or dust from the basket.
- Airflow is one of the most important factors that helps even cooking. It is because air circulation promotes equal heat at all sides of the pot. If your basket blocks the airflow, you may not get efficient cooking, damaging your appliance. Therefore, make sure your device has enough ventilation to avoid damage.

Mistakes to Avoid when Using an Air Fryer for the First Time

Preparing a perfect meal in an air fryer requires practice. Therefore, many new cooks make mistakes when cooking meals in air fryers. You must avoid these common mistakes while cooking food in an air fryer.

Cooking Food in an Unheated basket

Preheating an air fryer is crucial. It allows the recipe to cook to perfection when you place any food item in the basket. Putting any food item in the basket without preheating the appliance will take longer, and your meal may not cook thoroughly, especially when preparing beef or chicken.

Not Shaking the Basket

When cooking in an air fryer, it is crucial to shake the basket to allow the food to cook evenly. If you forget to shake the basket, your food may overcook from one side and undercook from the other. Shaking the basket is easy, but many first-time cooks often forget it. Therefore, set a timer on your phone to remind you to shake the basket.

Using a Dirty Air Fryer

The best way to enjoy an ideally air-fried meal is to ensure the basket is clean. Make sure you take extra care about cleaning the appliance after each use. It may sound complex and time-consuming, but keeping your appliance clean before you place meals is crucial for health. Moreover, cleaning the fryer from the inside doesn't take long; all you need is 5 minutes at most!

So, next time you prepare any meal in your air fryer, ensure you do not make these mistakes.

How do You Clean an Air Fryer?

Cleaning the air fryer after frying chicken, fries, or baking pizza is necessary. A thorough cleaning helps the appliance get rid of the grease and makes maintenance of the device easier. Let us guide you on how to clean your air fryer within no time.

Things you will need:

- Baking soda
- Microfiber cloths or cotton
- Non-abrasive sponge
- A toothbrush or soft-bristled brush
- Dish soap

Turn off and unplug your air fryer:

Switch off the appliance and unplug it. Leave the air fryer until it cools down. It may take half an hour to cool or quicker if you remove its basket or pan from the machine.

Wipe the machine

Use a damp microfiber cloth or cotton to wipe the outside of the machine. Once done, dip the non-abrasive sponge in hot water to clean the inside of the device.

Remove the food particles

If any hard stuck food particle does not come off from the surface or body of the appliance, make a paste of baking soda using water and rub the dirty spots with a soft brush or non-abrasive sponge. Wipe it using a microfiber cloth or cotton.

Wash the pan and the basket

Many air fryer companies claim their appliances to be dishwasher safe. You need to place them in the dishwasher and run your regular cycle. If your air fryer is not dishwasher-safe, cleaning the pan and the basket is easy and does not take much time. Use warm and mild detergent to wash the fryer and dry it with a lint-free soft towel.

Soak the pan and the basket

If harsh food particles are stuck on the pan or basket, soak them in hot water for ten minutes. Using a non-abrasive sponge, clean the surfaces to remove the hard-stuck residue. Repeat until your appliance is free from the entire residue.

Dry all the parts

Before reassembling your appliance, ensure all the parts are dry, and there are no water droplets inside the machine. Drying the pan, basket, and central unit is essential, especially before reassembling them.

Air Fryers Safety Tips

Air fryers have become immensely popular due to their numerous benefits. With little to no oil, you can quickly fry and cook meals. Air fryers have become a go-to option for people who are on a diet or prefer healthy eating.

However, these appliances come with a set of safety hazards and precautions. Here are some preventive measures you must take when using an air fryer.

Read the manual

Go through the instructions mentioned in the manual guide before using the appliance. Air fryers can get extremely hot. Therefore, to understand its functionality, it is crucial to know everything about the appliance before plugging it in.

Do not overcrowd the basket

When cooking meals in an air fryer, ensure you do not overcrowd the food basket. Every air fryer can fit different numbers of fillets or other food items. Make sure you do not place more than its capacity because overcrowding may lead to severe accidents.

Unplug the cord after use

Keeping the plug on after using the appliance can lead to accidents. Therefore, you must immediately unplug the cord after using the appliance to avoid risking your life.

Avoid using too much the oil

The primary purpose of air fryers is to cook meals without excessive oil. Air fryers are a blessing for people who want to enjoy crispy food without too much oil. Some recipes may require a tiny amount of oil to prepare a delicious meal. Therefore, add only the amount asked and avoid adding a lot of oil as it may cause a fire.

CHAPTER 1: BREAKFAST RECIPES

Herb-roasted Cauliflower

Total time: 24 minutes

Preparation time: 4 minutes

Cooking time: 20 minutes

Ingredients required:

- 375g cauliflower florets
- 150g sesame oil
- 6g onion powder
- 6g garlic powder
- 6g thyme
- 6g sage
- 6g rosemary
- Sea salt and cracked black pepper to taste
- 6g paprika

Serving:2

Calories: 118

Protein: 4.7g

Carbs: 8.6g

Fat: 8.2g

Fibre: 2g

Directions:

1. Start by preheating your Air Fryer to 400 degrees F.
2. Toss the cauliflower with the remaining ingredients; toss to coat well.
3. Cook for 12 minutes, shaking the cooking basket halfway through the cooking time. They will crisp up as they cool. Bon appétit!

Air Fryer Bacon And Eggs

Total time: 20 minutes

Preparation time: 5 minutes

Cooking time: 15 minutes

Ingredients required:

- 8g bread crumbs
- 8g bacon bits
- 4 eggs
- 192g water

Serving: 4

Calories: 92

Protein: 6g

Carbs: 0g

Fat: 7g

Fibre: 0 g

Directions:

1. Preheat the air fryer to 270 degrees F.
2. Place bread crumbs and bacon in a bowl. Shake to coat evenly then place on a rack. Place eggs on the rack and spray with cooking oil.
3. Cook for 16-18 minutes or until yolk is cooked through and the whites are cooked but not over cooked.
4. Immediately cut off the top of the egg and scoop out. Place eggs in a bowl of cold water.

Air Fryer Chicken Courgette Fritters

Total time: 50 minutes

Preparation time: 35 minutes

Cooking time: 15 minutes

Ingredients required:

- 200g minced chicken breast meat (or other cut of meat)
- 320ml egg whites
- 160ml chicken stock (or water)
- 2 (100g each) peeled and grated courgette (squeeze excess liquid from courgette)
- 1g nutmeg powder
- 2g paprika powder
- 2g garlic, crushed
- 1.6g white onion powder
- 1g salt
- 2g pepper

Serving: 4

Calories: 344

Protein: 17g

Carbs: 31g

Fat: 9g

Fibre: 6g

Directions:

1. Combine the ingredients for all the spices in a large bowl. Season with the spice mixture and set aside.
2. Add water to the bowl of your air fryer and place a plate on top to create a steam chamber. Place the courgette in the air fryer basket and cook for 20 minutes at 170C under Low fan speed.
3. While courgette is cooking, add chicken meat, long grain white rice and seasonings in a large bowl. Mix well to coat each piece evenly with seasoning then set aside.
4. Transfer cooked courgette to a clean tea towel and pat dry to remove any excess moisture. Add the cooked courgette to the chicken bowl and toss well.
5. In a small bowl, whisk egg whites until lightly frothy. Stir in stock and add this mixture to the chicken and courgette mixture. Gently fold through without over mixing.
6. Cook in an air fryer basket for 10 minutes at 170C on Low fan speed until lightly golden brown on top. Serve immediately.

Yummy Brownies

Total time: 20 minutes

Preparation time: 10 minutes

Cooking time: 10 minutes

Ingredients required:

- 150g cocoa powder
- 19g baking powder
- 3g baking soda
- 150g unsweetened applesauce
- 6g liquid stevia
- 75g coconut oil, melted
- 225g ground almonds
- 3g tsp vanilla
- 75g unsweetened almond milk
- 63g almond butter
- 1.5g sea salt

Serving: 4

Calories: 344

Protein: 17g

Carbs: 31g

Fat: 9g

Fibre: 6g

Directions:

1. Preheat the air fryer to 350 F.
2. Grease the air fryer baking dish with cooking spray and set aside.
3. Mix almond flour, baking soda, cocoa powder, baking powder, and salt in a little kitchen bowl.
4. Add coconut oil and almond butter to a small bowl and microwave until melted.
5. Add sweetener, vanilla, almond milk, and applesauce to the coconut oil mixture and stir well.
6. Add dry ingredients to the wet ingredients and stir to combine.
7. Put batter into the prepared dish and place into the air fryer, and cook for 10 minutes.
8. Slice and serve.

Air Fryer Scrambled Eggs

Total time: 17 minutes

Preparation time: 5 minutes

Cooking time: 12 minutes

Ingredients required:

- 4 eggs
- 1g salt
- 4g butter, melted and slightly cooled (melted)

Serving: 4

Calories: 132

Protein: 8g

Carbs: 2g

Fat: 15g

Fibre: 0g

Directions:

1. Preheat the air fryer to 270 degrees F.
2. Place eggs in the air fryer, preferably on a wire rack, and cook for 12-15 minutes or until the whites are set but still soft.
3. Immediately cut off the top of the egg and scoop out. Place eggs in a bowl of cold water.

Air Fryer Sausage Biscuits

Total time: 20 minutes

Preparation time: 5 minutes

Cooking time: 15 minutes

Ingredients required:

- 140g pork breakfast sausage
- 50g butter, melted
- 125g flour, plus extra for dusting
- 2 eggs
- 6g salt
- 1g black pepper

Serving: 8

Calories: 394

Protein: 23g

Carbs: 33g

Fat: 18g

Fibre: 5g

Directions:

1. Crumble sausage and cook in a frying pan. Drain fat, set aside and keep warm.
2. Prepare preheat the air fryer to 300 degrees F. Mix all the dry ingredients in a bowl. Make a well in the centre of the mixture, add eggs and then melted butter, stir until fully combined. Add cooked sausage, mix well.
3. Place mixture on a baking tray and bake for approximately 15 minutes, or until golden brown.

Egg Salad with Asparagus and Spinach

Total time: 31 minutes

Preparation time: 6 minutes

Cooking time: 25 minutes

Ingredients required:

- 4 eggs
- 45g asparagus, chopped
- 250g baby spinach
- 62.5g mayonnaise
- 6g mustard
- 6g fresh lemon juice
- Sea salt and ground black pepper to taste

Serving: 4

Calories: 195

Protein: 5.8g

Carbs: 2.8g

Fat: 7.6g

Fibre: 2.6g

Directions:

1. Place the wire rack in the Air Fryer basket; lower the eggs onto the wire rack.
2. Cook at 0 degrees F for 15 minutes.
3. Transfer them to an ice-cold water bath to stop the cooking. Peel the eggs under cold running water; coarsely chop the hard-boiled eggs and set them aside.
4. Increase the temperature to 0 degrees F. Place your asparagus in the lightly greased Air Fryer basket.
5. Cook for minutes or until tender. Place in a nice salad bowl. Add the baby spinach.
6. In a mixing dish, thoroughly combine the remaining ingredients. Drizzle this dressing over the asparagus in the salad bowl and top with the chopped eggs. Bon appétit!

Air Fryer Pancakes With Blueberries

Total time: 24 minutes

Preparation time: 10 minutes

Cooking time: 14 minutes

Ingredients required:

- 50g plain flour
- 10g butter, melted and slightly cooled (melted)
- 2 eggs
- 75g milk, unsweetened vanilla or flavoured
- 1g salt
- 100g blueberries

Serving: 4
Calories: 132
Protein: 10g
Carbs: 14g
Fat: 9g
Fibre: 0g

Directions:

1. Preheat the air fryer to 270 degrees F. Pour the flour into a bowl and mix in the butter, eggs, milk, salt and vanilla or flavoured milk. Stir until it forms into a thin paste. Add more flour if the mixture is too runny.
2. Preheat pan on the stove and spray with oil. Lightly spoon mixture onto pan and cook until browned. Flip over and repeat with other side.
3. Add blueberries to the pancakes and enjoy.

Air Fryer Cinnamon Pancakes

Total time: 20 minutes

Preparation time: 5 minutes

Cooking time: 15 minutes

Ingredients required:

- 300g plain flour
- 4 eggs
- 1g black pepper
- 1.5g salt
- 1g cinnamon

Serving: 4

Calories: 154

Protein: 8g

Carbs: 14g

Fat: 9.7g

Fibre: 0g

Directions:

1. Preheat the air fryer to 270 degrees F. Pour the flour into a bowl and mix in the eggs, pepper, salt and cinnamon. Stir until it forms into a thin paste. Add more flour if the mixture is too runny.
2. Preheat pan on the stove and spray with oil. Lightly spoon mixture onto pan and cook until browned. Flip over and repeat with other side.

Easy Cheesy Broccoli

Total time: 31 minutes

Preparation time: 6 minutes

Cooking time: 25 minutes

Ingredients required:

- 42g grated yellow cheese
- 1 large-sized head of broccoli, stemmed and cut small florets
- 36ml canola oil
- 150g dried rosemary
- 150g dried basil
- Salt and ground black pepper to taste

Serving: 4

Calories: 152

Protein: 5.6g

Carbs: 3.6g

Fat: 13.5g

Fibre: 2g

Directions:

1. Bring a medium pan filled with lightly salted water to a boil. Then, boil the broccoli florets for about 3 minutes.
2. Drain the broccoli florets well; toss them with the canola oil, rosemary, basil, salt, and black pepper.
3. Set your air fryer to 0 degrees F; arrange the seasoned broccoli in the cooking basket; set the timer for 17 minutes. Toss the broccoli halfway through the cooking process.
4. Serve warm, topped with grated cheese, and enjoy!

CHAPTER 2: MAIN DISHES

Easy Air Fryer Rice With Mushrooms And Caramelized Onions

Total time: 25 minutes

Preparation time: 10 minutes

Cooking time: 15 minutes

Ingredients required:

- 250g basmati rice, uncooked
- 2g salt (add more if desired)
- 2g garlic powder
- 2g onion powder
- 2g parmesan cheese, grated

Serving: 4

Calories: 216

Protein: 5g

Carbs: 5g

Fat: 2g

Fibre: 0.5g

Directions:

1. Add salt and garlic powder to the air fryer-safe bowl. Mix well until combined.

2. Spread the uncooked rice on a baking tray lined with baking paper. Transfer to an air fryer at 180C and cook for 5 minutes or until the rice is lightly browned in colour (watch closely as it can burn easily). Remove from the air fryer and set aside. Cover the rice with cling film and allow to cool.

3. Combine all ingredients in a mixing bowl and mix well. Add the cooled rice to the mixing bowl and combine until it reaches your desired consistency. Season to taste with salt and pepper, if desired. Transfer to an airtight container for up to 4 days in the fridge.

Air Fryer Tuna and Courgette Tortillas

Total time: 45 minutes

Preparation time: 15 minutes

Cooking time: 30 minutes

Ingredients required:

- 3.5g salt
- 2g black pepper
- 1.3g sesame seeds, toasted and roughly chopped
- 1.3g garlic, toasted and roughly minced
- 1.3g paprika
- 500g courgette, sliced into thin rounds
- 50g green onions, chopped
- 125ml tomato ketchup (or tomato puree)
- 2g soy sauce powder
- 2g paprika
- 1g cumin

Serving: 4

Calories: 496

Protein: 24g

Carbs: 41g

Fat: 12g

Fibre: 1.8g

Directions:

1. Place salt, pepper and sesame seeds in the air fryer-safe bowl and mix well until combined. Set aside.
2. In your air fryer, add green onions with tomato ketchup to your air fryer-safe bowl and mix well. Add garlic, paprika and cumin to the bowl and stir until combined. Add courgette to the bowl and stir until well coated with tomato ketchup mixture. Set aside. Add tomatoes to a large bowl, add soy sauce and set aside.
3. In your air fryer, add tuna and courgette, pour over the tomato sauce mixture, drizzle over some water if required then cook at 170C for 12 minutes or until cooked through. Serve immediately with green salad and toasted brown rice or quinoa to serve as a side dish.

Air Fryer Macaroni and Cheese

Total time: 35 minutes

Preparation time: 10 minutes

Cooking time: 25 minutes

Ingredients required:

- 400g macaroni,
  cooked according to the packet instructions
- 60ml dry white wine (or chicken stock)
- 1.2g salt
- 1.2g black pepper
- 120ml double cream
- 200g cheddar cheese, grated,
  plus extra for sprinkling on top if desired

Serving: 4
Calories: 397
Protein: 25.5g
Carbs: 3g
Fat: 18g
Fibre: 1.2g

Directions:

1. Season the macaroni with salt and pepper then set aside. Whisk together cream and wine or stock until smooth or pour into a bowl and add cheese a few strands at a time then whisk to combine. Set aside.
2. In your air fryer, add cooked macaroni to the air fryer-safe bowl, pour over cream mixture and cook at 170C for 10 minutes or until cheese is melted.
3. Serve immediately with chopped chives if desired.

Air Fryer Cottage Pie

Total time: 25 minutes

Preparation time: 5 minutes

Cooking time: 20 minutes

Ingredients required:

- 2g salt
- 2g pepper
- 3g paprika
- 1.5g nutmeg
- 2.5g olive oil
- 2 (720g each) minced beef (or lamb)
- 1.5g white onion, finely chopped

Serving: 4

Calories: 401

Protein: 21g

Carbs: 16g

Fat: 7g

Fibre: 2g

Directions:

1. Season mince with salt, pepper and paprika. Set aside.
2. Heat oil in a large frying pan over medium high heat.
3. Cook mince for 3 minutes until browned then set aside in a bowl.
4. Add white onion to the frying pan and cook until softened and lightly browned.
5. Return mince to the frying pan along with all other ingredients and stir well to combine.
6. Bring to the boil then reduce heat and simmer until thickened (approximately 10 minutes). Set aside.

Air Fryer Lunch Pork and Potatoes

Total time: 25 minutes

Preparation time: 10 minutes

Cooking time: 25 minutes

Ingredients required:

- 500g potatoes, sliced into thin rounds
- 500g pork, thinly sliced into bite-size pieces
- 3g salt
- 1g black pepper
- 2.8g paprika
- 2.7g garlic powder
- 2.7g oregano
- 1.7g cumin

Serving: 4

Calories: 345

Protein: 20g

Carbs: 46g

Fat: 6.5g

Fibre: 4g

Directions:

1. Place salt, pepper and paprika in the air fryer-safe bowl and mix well until combined. Set aside.
2. Place garlic powder, oregano and cumin in the air fryer-safe bowl and mix well until combined. Set aside.
3. In your air fryer, add potatoes to the air fryer-safe bowl, drizzle over some oil (if required) and cook at 170C for 10 minutes or until golden brown in colour.
4. After 10 minutes, add pork to the bowl and continue cooking until pork is cooked through. Serve immediately with a salad and toasted brown rice or quinoa as a side dish.

Cheese Ravioli and Marinara Sauce

Total time: 32 minutes

Preparation time: 8 minutes

Cooking time: 25 minutes

Ingredients required:

- 250g basil leaves, roughly chopped (or 1 tsp dried basil)
- 2.8g paprika but you can use smoked paprika if desired
- 2g celery seeds
- 2g black pepper
- 250ml tomato passata
- 4.5g salt
- 1.3g pepper
- 6g oregano, dried and finely chopped
- 6g garlic powder
- 375g cheese ravioli (or you can use your desired filling)

Serving: 4

Calories: 290

Protein: 18.5g

Carbs: 36g

Fat: 3.2g

Fibre: 6.3g

Directions:

1. Combine salt, pepper and garlic powder in the air fryer-safe bowl then set aside. Place oregano and celery seeds in the air fryer-safe bowl and mix well until combined. Set aside.
2. Place paprika, black pepper and basil leaves in the air fryer-safe bowl and mix together. Set aside. In your air fryer, cook marinara sauce at 170C for 5 minutes or until reduced by half. Set aside.
3. Place ravioli in the air fryer-safe bowl, pour over some oil (if required) and cook at 170C for 10 minutes or until cooked through. After 10 minutes, add tomato passata to the bowl, drizzle over some oil (if required) and continue cooking until ravioli is cooked.
4. Place sauce in a serving bowl, add ravioli and serve with toasted brown rice or quinoa as a side dish.

Air Fryer Coconut and Chicken Casserole

Total time: 30 minutes

Preparation time: 10 minutes

Cooking time: 20 minutes

Ingredients required:

- 4 x 100g chicken, sliced into bite-size pieces
- 2.8g salt
- 1.7g black pepper
- 1.7g paprika
- 2.7g garlic powder
- 2.7g oregano
- 1.7g cumin
- 500ml coconut milk

Serving: 1

Calories: 373

Protein: 29.5g

Carbs: 8g

Fat: 24g

Fibre: 1g

Directions:

1. Combine salt, pepper and garlic powder in the air fryer-safe bowl then set aside.
2. Place oregano, cumin and paprika in the air fryer-safe bowl and mix well until combined. Set aside.
3. In your air fryer, add chicken and coconut milk to the air fryer-safe bowl.
4. Cook at 170C for 8 minutes or until chicken is cooked through. Set aside.
5. Place chicken in a bowl and pour over marinade, mix well until chicken is covered then serve immediately with toasted brown rice or quinoa as a side dish.

Air Fryer Prawns Fajitas

Total time: 40 minutes

Preparation time: 10 minutes

Cooking time: 30 minutes

Ingredients required:

- 450g chicken breast, thinly sliced into bite sized pieces
- 2.7g chilli powder
- 400g raw king prawns, peeled and deveined
- 2g salt
- 1.7g black pepper
- 310ml tomato sauce or salsa
- 1.5g paprika (plus extra for sprinkling)
- 2.5g garlic powder
- 2.5g oregano, dried and finely chopped
- 1.7g cumin seed (plus extra for sprinkling)

Serving: 4
Calories: 654
Protein: 53g
Carbs: 65g
Fat: 13.3g
Fibre: 6.8g

Directions:

1. Preheat the air fryer to 180 degrees Celsius/350 degrees Fahrenheit. Once hot, place the chicken breast in a single layer on to a wire rack. Set aside for 5 minutes until white meat is no longer pink.
2. Add the tomato sauce and spices to a small bowl and mix to combine. Set aside for later.
3. Once the chicken is ready, add it and the prawns onto a large plate (or directly inside of the air fryer basket). Pour the tomato sauce and spices over the chicken and prawns and toss to combine.
4. Cook for 20 minutes. Serve with rice or quinoa, green vegetables and lemon wedges.

Air fryer Prawn with Lemon and Pepper

Total time: 48 minutes

Preparation time: 10 minutes

Cooking time: 38 minutes

Ingredients required:

- 350g prawns, peeled and deveined
- 2g salt
- 250ml extra-virgin olive oil (plus extra if needed)
- 2g black pepper
- 1.5g paprika (plus extra for sprinkling)
- 2.5g garlic powder
- 1.7g cayenne pepper
- 10g parsley

Serving: 2

Calories: 370

Protein: 31g

Carbs: 9.7g

Fat: 22g

Fibre: 1.3g

Directions:

1. Add garlic powder, salt and pepper in the air fryer-safe bowl, mix well until combined. Set aside.
2. Place olive oil in a small bowl then add paprika, cumin and cayenne pepper to it and mix until combined. Set aside.
3. Place shrimp in your air fryer on medium heat. Cook at 170C for 8 minutes or until pink is softened and cooked through.
4. After 8 minutes, remove shrimp from the air fryer and place aside.
5. Place oil in the air fryer-safe bowl then place on top of the shrimp. Cook for a further 1 to 2 minutes or until fragrant.
6. Remove oil from the air fryer and set aside with fried shrimp to cool slightly. Garnish with parsley then serve immediately with a side salad or toasted brown rice or quinoa.

Air Fryer Fried Rice

Total time: 53 minutes

Preparation time: 15 minutes

Cooking time: 38 minutes

Ingredients required:

Serving: 4

Calories: 326

Protein: 3.6g

Carbs: 11g

Fat: 32g

Fibre: 0.5g

- 100g white rice, cooked
- 3g paprika (plus extra for sprinkling)
- 2g dried oregano, finely chopped
- 2.5g garlic powder (plus extra for sprinkling)
- 250ml olive oil (use more if needed)
- 2g salt
- 2g black pepper
- 3g fresh parsley, chopped

Directions:

1. Place salt, garlic powder and paprika in the air fryer-safe bowl then set aside.
2. Add olive oil in the air fryer-safe bowl, cook at 170C for 1 minute or until fragrant. Add in parsley then set aside.
3. Place rice on a large plate (or directly inside of the air fryer basket).
4. Sprinkle over paprika, garlic powder and oregano then toss well to combine.
5. Cook for 20 minutes or until golden brown in colour. Set aside with spices to cool slightly.
6. Once rice is ready, divide between 2 plates then drizzle over oil and parsley. Sprinkle with extra paprika and oregano. Serve with a side salad or toasted brown rice or quinoa.

CHAPTER 3: POULTRY RECIPES

Air Fryer Chicken Curry

Total time: 30 minutes

Preparation time: 10 minutes

Cooking time: 20 minutes

Ingredients required:

- 4 x 115g skinless boneless chicken breasts
- 300ml coconut milk
- 100ml Greek yogurt
- 100ml tomato pure
- 50g spinach, roughly chopped
- 1.5g salt
- 0.5g black pepper
- 3g turmeric

Serving: 4

Calories: 419

Protein: 32.5g

Carbs: 18.7g

Fat: 15g

Fibre: 4.6g

Directions:

1. Pour tomato puree, coconut milk and yogurts into an air fryer-safe bowl.
2. Season with salt, pepper and turmeric. Stir well to combine ingredients.
3. Place chicken breast into the air fryer basket in a single layer and cook at 170C for 10 minutes.
4. Remove from the air fryer and stir through chopped spinach and allow to stand for 30 seconds for the spinach to wilt slightly.
5. Serve chicken curry with rice or naan breads.

Air Fryer Chicken Nuggets

Total time: 25 minutes

Preparation time: 5 minutes

Cooking time: 20 minutes

Ingredients required:

- 4 (115g each) skinless boneless chicken breasts (or other cut of chicken)
- 2.2g parmesan cheese, grated
- 300ml coconut milk
- 1 egg white
- 100ml Greek yogurt
- 1 lime, zest and juice
- 0.5g Sriracha sauce (optional)
- 1.5g salt
- 1.3g pepper
- 2g sesame seeds, toasted and roughly chopped
- 2g garlic, toasted and roughly minced

Serving: 4

Calories: 388

Protein: 17g

Carbs: 19.3g

Fat: 13g

Fibre: 2.5g

Directions:

1. Pour tomato puree, coconut milk and yogurts into an air fryer-safe bowl. Season with salt, pepper and turmeric. Stir well to combine ingredients.
2. Place chicken breast into the air fryer basket in a single layer and cook at 170C for 15 minutes or until cooked through.
3. Remove from the air fryer and set aside on a serving dish.
4. Whisk egg white in a large bowl until frothy. Pour over the chicken breasts and toss well to coat each chicken piece evenly.
5. In an air fryer-safe bowl, add chicken pieces with egg white and cook at 170C for 10 minutes or until lightly golden brown. Remove from the fryer and serve immediately.
6. To serve: divide chicken nuggets between four serving containers and store in the fridge for 4 hours to allow any excess moisture to be absorbed by the chicken.

Air Fryer Chicken with Pineapple and Chilli Jam

Total time: 20 minutes

Preparation time: 5 minutes

Cooking time: 15 minutes

Ingredients required:

- 200ml pineapple jam (or blueberry or apricot)
- 100g can of chopped pineapple in juice
  (or similar canned fruit).
- 2g salt, to taste
- 2.7g pepper, to taste
- 2.7g garlic powder, to taste
- 200g chicken breasts, sliced into 4 portions (optional)
- 1.5g white onion powder, to taste

Serving: 4

Calories: 571

Protein: 29g

Carbs: 31g

Fat: 33g

Fibre: 4.8g

Directions:

1. In a bowl, mix all spices together. Add chicken and set aside. Place oil in the air fryer basket and place a plate on top to create a steam chamber.
2. Place chicken in the air fryer basket and cook for 5 minutes at 170C under Low fan speed. When done, remove from the air fryer basket and set aside until ready to serve.
3. When ready to serve, place pineapple jam in the same bowl used to marinate chicken. Add the chopped pineapple and mix with a spoon until well combined.
4. When done, remove air fryer basket, transfer to a plate and top with chicken. Serve immediately with fresh chopped herbs.

Lemon Pepper Chicken Wings

Total time: 24 minutes

Preparation time: 8 minutes

Cooking time: 16 minutes

Ingredients required:

- 454g chicken wings
- 3g lemon pepper
- 75g olive oil
- 3g salt , to taste

Serving: 3

Calories: 291

Protein: 15.5g

Carbs: 2g

Fat: 24.6g

Fibre: 1.2g

Directions:

1. Add chicken wings to the large mixing bowl.
2. Add remaining ingredients over chicken and toss well to coat.
3. Place chicken wings in the air fryer basket.
4. Cook chicken wings for 8 minutes at 0 F.
5. Turn chicken wings to another side and cook for 8 minutes more.
6. Serve and enjoy.

Air Fryer Smoked Turkey Wings

Total time: 35 minutes

Preparation time: 15 minutes

Cooking time: 20 minutes

Ingredients required:

- 300g smoked turkey wings, cut into 4 pieces each
- 15g unsalted butter
- 30g hot chili oil
- 2g salt
- 2g black pepper
- 1g juniper berries

Serving: 4

Calories: 385

Protein: 21g

Carbs: 19.4g

Fat: 19g

Fibre: 3g

Directions:

1. Heat the air fryer to 190C. Combine hot chili oil, butter and juniper berries in an air fryer-safe bowl. Gently season with salt and pepper.
2. Place turkey wings into the air fryer basket in a single layer and cook at 170C for 20 minutes until cooked through.
3. Remove from the air fryer and brush turkey wings with the chili oil mixture. Serve.

Rosemary Honey Air-Fried Duck Breasts with Bacon

Total time: 25 minutes

Preparation time: 10 minutes

Cooking time: 15 minutes

Ingredients required:

- 1.2g ground cinnamon
- 0.5g Chinese five spice powder
- 400g tin peach, drained and chopped
- 4 x 150g duck breast, skin on, scored to ensure a perfect shape
- 1.5g salt
- 3g black pepper
- 2g ground nutmeg
- 50g rindless smoked back bacon, cut into4 pieces each

Serving: 4

Calories: 487

Protein: 29.5g

Carbs: 17.5g

Fat: 40g

Fibre: 3.2g

Directions:

1. Heat the air fryer to 190C.
2. Place duck breasts skin side down in the air fryer basket and cook at 170C for 15 minutes until cooked through. Remove from the air fryer and allow to rest for 5 minutes.
3. While duck breasts are cooking, make the sauce by placing peach, bacon and Chinese five spice powder into an air fryer-safe bowl and cook at 170C for 5 minutes.
4. Remove from the air fryer and combine with duck breasts.
5. Serve with rice or couscous.

Crispy Air Fryer Duck Breast

Total time: 20 minutes

Preparation time: 10 minutes

Cooking time: 10 minutes

Ingredients required:

- 4 x 150g duck breast, skin on and scored to ensure a perfect shape
- 2g salt
- 1.5g black pepper
- 1.5g chili powder
- 1.5g cumin

Serving: 4

Calories: 418

Protein: 42g

Carbs: 3.8g

Fat: 20g

Fibre: 1.6g

Directions:

1. Heat the air fryer to 190C. In a bowl combine salt, black pepper, chili powder and cumin. Season with additional salt if necessary.
2. Place duck breasts skin side down in the air fryer basket and cook at 170C for 10 minutes until cooked through.
3. Remove from the air fryer and allow to rest for 5 minutes.
4. While duck breasts are cooking, make the sauce by combining peach, bacon and Chinese five spice powder into an air fryer-safe bowl and cook at 170C for 5 minutes.
5. Remove from the air fryer, season with additional salt if necessary, spoon sauce over duck and serve with rice or couscous.

Shaking Tarragon Chicken Tenders

Total time: 25 minutes

Preparation time: 10 minutes

Cooking time: 15 minutes

Ingredients required:

- 125ml dried tarragon
- 75g butter
- 450g chicken
- Salt and pepper to taste

Serving: 4	
Calories: 706	
Protein: 33g	
Carbs: 22.5g	
Fat: 54.3g	
Fibre: 1g	

Directions:

1. Preheat the air fryer to 390 F. Lay an X 12-inch cut of foil on a flat surface. Place the chicken on the foil, sprinkle the tarragon on both, and share the butter onto both breasts. Sprinkle with salt and pepper.

2 Loosely wrap the foil around the breasts to enable airflow. Place the wrapped chicken in the basket and cook for 1minutes. Remove the chicken and carefully unwrap the foil. Serve with the sauce extract and steamed veggies.

3.Serve and enjoy.

Air Fryer Cornish Hens Recipe

Total time: 30 minutes

Preparation time: 10 minutes

Cooking time: 20 minutes

Ingredients required:

- 1g chives, chopped (optional)
- 50g butter
- 4 x 50ml Greek yogurt
- 4 x 35g Manchego cheese, grated
- 1.5g salt
- 0.5g black pepper
- 1g paprika powder
- 4 x 115g Cornish hens, skin on and split down the middle

Serving: 4

Calories: 599

Protein: 54.7g

Carbs: 8g

Fat: 37g

Fibre: 0.9g

Directions:

1. Heat the air fryer to 170C. Combine black pepper, paprika powder and chives (if using) in an air fryer-safe bowl.
2. Season with salt if necessary. Place Cornish game hens into the air fryer basket in a single layer and cook at 170C for 15 minutes. Remove from the air fryer and allow to rest for 5 minutes.
3. While game hens are cooking, place butter into an air fryer-safe bowl and whisk until melted using a hand held whisk or a stick blender.
4. Place Greek yogurt in a small sauce pan over low heat and stir constantly until warm and melted.
5. Combine yogurt, butter, Manchego cheese together in an air fryer-safe bowl and mix well with a spatula until smooth.
6. Place hens on the serving plate and spoon sauce over game hens. Serve with pita bread and salad or couscous.

Honey Duck Breasts

Total time: 30 minutes

Preparation time: 10 minutes

Cooking time: 20 minutes

Ingredients required:

- 1.5g salt
- 2g ground cinnamon
- 0.5g grated nutmeg
- 3g rosemary leaves
- 50ml honey
- 6 x 150g skin-on duck breasts, scored to ensure a perfect shape

Serving: 4

Calories: 371

Protein: 28g

Carbs: 7.6g

Fat: 18g

Fibre: 1.6g

Directions:

1. Heat the air fryer to 190C. Combine honey, nutmeg, salt and cinnamon in an air fryer-safe bowl. Mix well to combine.
2. Add duck breast into the mixture and turn to coat evenly. Place duck breast in the air fryer basket in a single layer and cook at 170C for 15 minutes until cooked through.
3. Remove from the air fryer and allow to rest for 5 minutes.
4. Serve with potato mash and your favourite greens.

Turkey Quarters and Veggies

Total time: 25 minutes

Preparation time: 10 minutes

Cooking time: 15 minutes

Ingredients required:

- 1.5g salt
- 2g black pepper
- 50ml soy sauce
- 300g turkey quarters, skin on
- 250g green beans, ends snapped off and blanched
- 1 white onion, sliced
- 2g of garlic, crushed

Serving: 4

Calories: 306

Protein: 64g

Carbs: 6.5g

Fat: 4g

Fibre: 3.5g

Directions:

1. Heat the air fryer to 190C. Rub turkey quarters with soy sauce and season with salt and pepper.
2. Place in the air fryer basket in a single layer over green beans and cook at 170C for 15 minutes until cooked through.
3. Remove from the air fryer and allow to rest for 5 minutes. Remove the skin from turkey quarters and serve topped with fresh onion and garlic.
4. Serve and enjoy.

CHAPTER 4: MEAT RECIPES

Air-Fryer Taco Puffs

Total time: 30 minutes

Preparation time: 15 minutes

Cooking time: 15 minutes

Ingredients required:

- 450g ground beef
- 120g shredded cheddar cheese
- 28g McCormick's Taco Season
- 160g corn flakes, crushed

Serving: 4

Calories: 330

Protein: 23g

Carbs: 34g

Fat: 15g

Fibre: 1g

Directions:

1. Brown the beef on the stovetop in a large skillet and drain any excess fat.
2. Spray the inner basket of the air fryer with oil and add the beef, cover and cook on high for 5 minutes.
3. Add in taco seasoning and part of the cheese and mix well.
4. Set the air fryer to 375°F (190°C) for 5 minutes.
5. Add the corn flakes and continue to cook on high for about 5 minutes until the corn flakes are crispy and the dish is hot and melted.

Air Fryer Pork Chops

Total time: 23 minutes

Preparation time: 15 minutes

Cooking time: 8 minutes

Ingredients required:

- 1 large egg, beaten lightly
- 30mil pure maple syrup
- 15g Dijon mustard
- 3.6g paprika
- 2.3g fresh black pepper
- 200g pork chops, sliced into thin strips
- 20g butter, melted

Serving: 4

Calories: 200

Protein: 33g

Carbs: 1g

Fat: 12g

Fibre: 0g

Directions:

1. Add the maple syrup, paprika, black pepper and egg. Stir to mix well. Place the pork chop strips into a ziplock bag and then add in the marinade sauce.
2. Combine everything well to ensure that each strip is well-coated with the sauce. Marinate for one hour in the fridge.
3. Soak wood skewers with water for 30 minutes.
4. Place skewers in the air fryer basket and cook on high for 8 minutes. Turn the meat occasionally so that it cooks evenly.

Air Fryer Bacon-Wrapped Hot Dogs

Total time: 25 minutes

Preparation time: 15 minutes

Cooking time: 10 minutes

Ingredients required:

- 300g hot dogs
- 10g bacon, cut into small bits
- 20g sunflower seeds
- 1.5g paprika
- 3.6g fresh black pepper

Serving: 4

Calories: 260

Protein: 14g

Carbs: 8g

Fat: 16g

Fibre: 3g

Directions:

1. Trim the hot dogs of any excess skin and cut them into thin strips.
2. Combine all of the ingredients together in a ziplock bag and mix well to ensure that each ingredient is evenly coated. Marinate for one hour in the fridge.
3. Soak wood skewers with water for 30 minutes.
4. Place the hot dog strips onto the skewers and cook in an air fryer for about 10 minutes.

Air Fryer Juicy Steak Bites

Total time: 25 minutes

Preparation time: 15 minutes

Cooking time: 10 minutes

Ingredients required:

- 450g pork tenderloin, cut into small stripes
- 20g butter, melted (divided)
- 33ml olive oil (divided)
- 3.5g paprika (divided)
- 2g fresh black pepper (divided)
- 1.5g garlic powder (divided)
- 1.5g onion powder (divided)

Serving: 4

Calories: 230

Protein: 30g

Carbs: 4g

Fat: 9g

Fibre: 1g

Directions:

1. Place the pork strips in a ziplock bag and add in half of the butter, half of the olive oil, half of the paprika, half of the black pepper, half of the garlic powder and onion powder.
2. Massage well to ensure that each piece is well-coated by the seasonings.
3. Marinate for 1 hour in the fridge.
4. Soak wood skewers with water for 30 minutes.
5. Place the pork strips on the skewers and cook in an air fryer for about 10 minutes.
6. Turn the meat occasionally so that it cooks evenly.

Air Fryer Meat Loaf

Total time: 30 minutes

Preparation time: 10 minutes

Cooking time: 20 minutes

Ingredients required:

- 100g mozzarella cheese, grated
- 63.1ml homemade tomato sauce
- 50g parsley, chopped
- 1.5kg ground beef

Serving: 6
Calories: 300
Protein: 52g
Carbs: 4g
Fat: 14g
Fibre: 0g

Directions:

1. Preheat the air fryer to 375°F (190°C). Combine all of the ingredients together in a large bowl.
2. Spoon the mixture into a loaf pan. Cover with aluminum foil.
3. Bake in the air fryer for 20 minutes. Remove from the air fryer and remove and discard the aluminum foil. Bake for another 10 minutes.

Air Fryer Bacon Cheeseburgers

Total time: 25 minutes

Preparation time: 15 minutes

Cooking time: 10 minutes

Ingredients required:

- 125g package cheese, sliced
- 60g tomato, chopped
- 35g onion, chopped
- 20g bread crumbs
- 1.5kg ground beef

Serving: 4

Calories: 440

Protein: 44g

Carbs: 4g

Fat: 20g

Fibre: 0g

Directions:

1. Preheat the air fryer to 375°F (190°C). Combine all of the ingredients together in a large bowl.
2. Spray the inner basket of the air fryer with oil and add in half of the beef. Cover and cook for about 4 minutes on high.
3. Add more bread crumbs as needed, until you achieve your desired thickness.
4. Turn each burner half way through cooking time to ensure even cooking. Let cool before serving.

Air Fryer Beefy Swiss Bundles

Total time: 22 minutes

Preparation time: 10 minutes

Cooking time: 12 minutes

Ingredients required:

- 60g bread crumbs, panko style
- 40g cheddar cheese, grated
- 20g parsley, chopped finely (divided)
- 1.5kg ground beef (divided)

Serving: 4

Calories: 340

Protein: 28g

Carbs: 6g

Fat: 16g

Fibre: 1g

Directions:

1. Grate the cheese and soak each slice in water. Drain well and pat dry. Combine all of the ingredients together in a large bowl and mix well.
2. Divide into 4 portions, making sure that each portion has an even amount of meat, cheese, onions and parsley.
3. Prepare the air fryer to cook at 375°F (190°C).
4. Place one portion onto each cornflake ring.
5. Cook for about 12 minutes until the center is cooked.
6. Turn each burner half way through cooking time to ensure even cooking.

Air Fryer Lamb Burger

Total time: 25 minutes

Preparation time: 15 minutes

Cooking time: 10 minutes

Ingredients required:

- 2.5kg lamb mince
- 200ml tomato ketchup
- 40g sundried tomato, chopped finely
- 80g bread crumbs (divided)
- 11ml olive oil (divided)

Serving: 6
Calories: 320
Protein: 35g
Carbs: 6g
Fat: 13g
Fibre: 1g

Directions:

1. Preheat the air fryer to 375°F (190°C). Place the lamb mince into a large bowl.
2. Add in half of the onion, half of the sundried tomato, half of the bread crumbs, half of the olive oil and half of the ketchup.
3. Massage well to ensure that every piece is coated with all ingredients.
4. Place one portion onto each cornflake ring and cook for about 10 minutes until cooked through.
5. Turn each burner half way through cooking time to ensure even cooking.

Air Fryer Ribeye Steak

Total time: 25 minutes

Preparation time: 15 minutes

Cooking time: 10 minutes

Ingredients required:

- 2.5kg ribeye steak, boneless, trimmed of excess fat and sliced into two inch slabs
- 66.7ml olive oil (divided)
- 250ml bbq sauce, homemade or store bought (divided)

Serving: 4

Calories: 420

Protein: 50g

Carbs: 18g

Fat: 11g

Fibre: 0g

Directions:

1. Preheat the air fryer to 375°F (190°C). Place the ribeye strips onto a parchment lined baking sheet.
2. Brush with half of the olive oil and then turn each strip half way through. Bake for 5 minutes on each side.
3. Prepare the air fryer to cook at 375°F (190°C).
4. Place one strip onto each cornflake ring and then brush with half of the bbq sauce.
5. Cook for another 2 minutes on each side.
6. Turn each burner half way through cooking time to ensure even cooking.

Air Fryer Garlic Butter Steaks

Total time: 23 minutes

Preparation time: 15 minutes

Cooking time: 8 minutes

Ingredients required:

- 880g beef fillet, rib eye or tenderloin steak, trimmed of excess fat and thinly sliced into two inch strips
- 320g butter, soft (divided)
- 20g fresh parsley, chopped finely (divided)
- 2.5g fresh basil (divided)

Serving: 4

Calories: 480

Protein: 51g

Carbs: 16g

Fat: 14g

Fibre: 3g

Directions:

1. Preheat the air fryer to 375°F (190°C). Place the beef strip onto a parchment lined baking sheet.
2. Place half of the butter on top of each strip and gently massage to coat.
3. Add in half of the parsley and basil, season well. Half way through cooking time, add in remaining butter as needed until you reach desired consistency.
4. Prepare the air fryer to cook at 375°F (190°C).
5. Place half of the steak strips on each cornflake ring and cook for about 4 minutes until cooked through.
6. Turn each burner half way through cooking time to ensure even cooking.

CHAPTER 5: SEAFOOD RECIPES

Prawns with Lemon and Pepper Sauce

Total time: 23 minutes

Preparation time: 10 minutes

Cooking time: 15 minutes

Ingredients required:

- 12g butter, melted
- 50g onion, diced small
- 60ml of the stock to deglaze the pan with (spoonful)
- 270g prawns, deveined and peeled

Serving: 4

Calories: 534

Protein: 26.8g

Carbs: 30.3g

Fat: 13.2g

Fibre: 3.7g

Directions:

1. Combine the butter and onion in a medium-sized frying pan over medium heat. Melt the butter and allow to caramelise without browning.
2. Continuously stir the onion and butter until all of the onion has been added to the pan and it is nice and golden brown. Slowly add the stock, allowing it to deglaze the pan and become a sauce.
3. Stir in the Prawns and cook until cooked through.
4. Transfer the Prawn pie to a serving platter and accompany with brown rice, fresh salad, and browned butter croutons.

Prawns Scampi with Spicy Pepper Sauce

Total time: 25 minutes

Preparation time: 10 minutes

Cooking time: 15 minutes

Ingredients required:

- 340g prawns, peeled, deveined and thawed
- 15ml olive oil
- 3g cloves garlic, minced fine
- 20g red onion, diced small
- 10g parsley leaves
- 10ml tomato paste
- 10ml balsamic vinegar

Serving: 4

Calories: 129

Protein: 21.8g

Carbs: 2.5g

Fat: 5.9g

Fibre: 0.4g

Directions:

1. Combine the olive oil, garlic and onion in a medium size frying pan over medium heat. Cook until the onion shrinks and becomes translucent (approx 3-5 minutes).
2. Add the tomato paste and balsamic vinegar; combine until aromatic (approx 3 minutes).
3. Add the Prawns and cook for another minute.
4. Transfer to a large serving plate, sprinkle with parsley leaves, serve with lemon wedges on the side to squeeze over if desired.

Air Fryer Fish Fillets with Chive Butter

Total time: 25 minutes

Preparation time: 10 minutes

Cooking time: 15 minutes

Ingredients required:

- 120g tilapia, cut into 2 inch x 1 inch pieces and patted dry
- 250ml of water
- 1.5g salt
- 20g chives, finely chopped

Serving: 4

Calories: 130

Protein: 22.3g

Carbs: 0g

Fat: 5.4g

Fibre:0.4g

Directions:

1. Combine the tilapia pieces and salt in a medium-sized mixing bowl. Cover with cold water and refrigerate for 30 minutes to bring down the temperature of the fish.
2. In a separate bowl, combine the chives and butter. Mix until fully combined and set aside for serving.
3. Remove the fish from the fridge; drain and pat dry with paper towels (do not rinse).
4. Skewer each portion of fish on wooden skewers or metal ones, depending on your preference (you don't want to use plastic as friction will lead to melting). I'll take a wild guess and say you will want to serve these with a fresh green salad.
5. Combine the water and/or oil in a medium-sized mixing bowl. Pour the liquid over the fish, making sure every piece is wet.
6. Cook in your air fryer at 370 degrees for 10-15 minutes (depending on if you'd like your fish crispy or tender). Flip after 5 minutes and brush with chive butter before serving (over steamed rice or a fresh green salad).

Air Fryer Teriyaki Salmon Fillets with Broccoli

Total time: 45 minutes

Preparation time: 15 minutes

Cooking time: 30 minutes

Ingredients required:

- 4 x 150g salmon fillets
- 60ml teriyaki sauce
- 60g brown sugar
- 15ml rice vinegar
- 250g broccoli, cut into florets

Serving: 4

Calories: 354

Protein: 29g

Carbs: 35g

Fat: 11g

Fibre: 4.5g

Directions:

1. Season the salmon with salt and pepper then set aside. Whisk together teriyaki sauce and brown sugar until smooth. Add a splash of water if it is too thick. Set aside.
2. In a large bowl, combine broccoli florets with rice vinegar and set aside.
3. In your air fryer, add salmon fillets and broccoli, pour over the teriyaki sauce mixture and cook at 170C for 15 minutes.

Tuna with Roasted Garlic and Hazelnuts

Total time: 25 minutes

Preparation time: 10 minutes

Cooking time: 15minutes

Ingredients required:

- 75ml of the stock from the hake
- 200g tuna fillet, cut into 1 inch x 1/2 inch pieces
- 20g hazelnuts, chopped
- 15g roasted and crushed garlic clove

Serving: 4

Calories: 455

Protein: 42.2g

Carbs: 9.7g

Fat: 12.7g

Fibre: 2g

Directions:

1. Combine all of the stock ingredients in a bowl, making sure to whisk in the hake slice at the end. Set aside for 5 minutes to allow the flavours to amalgamate.
2. Preheat your air fryer to 370 degrees.
3. Skewer the fish and roast in the air fryer.
4. Remove the hake from the stock and reserve the stock to make a sauce or to drizzle over your food.
5. Mix the roasted garlic and hazelnuts in a small bowl until well incorporated and set aside (be careful not to incorporate too much red pepper as this could alter the flavour).
6. Place the tuna on a plate and serve with brown rice, fresh salad, and roasted garlic hazelnuts.

Tarragon And Spring Onions Salmon

Total time: 23 minutes

Preparation time: 8 minutes

Cooking time: 15minutes

Ingredients required:

- 340ml salmon fillet
- 2 spring onions, chopped
- 75g ghee, melted
- 75g peppercorns
- 2.8g salt
- 2.8g ground black pepper
- 5.6g tarragon
- 2.8g dried cilantro

Serving: 4

Calories: 512

Protein: 19.9g

Carbs: 4.3g

Fat: 46.2g

Fibre: 7.2g

Directions:

1. Cut the salmon fillet into 4 servings. Then make the parchment pockets and place the fish fillets in the parchment pockets. Sprinkle the salmon with salt, ground black pepper, tarragon, and dried cilantro. Afterward, top the fish with spring onions, peppercorns, and ghee. Preheat the air fryer to 385F. Arrange the salmon pockets in the air fryer in one layer and cook them for minutes.

Air Fryer Salmon Teriyaki

Total time: 12 minutes

Preparation time: 4 minutes

Cooking time: 8 minutes

Ingredients required:

- 120ml teriyaki sauce (low-sodium)
- 60ml rice vinegar
- 60ml orange juice
- 400g wild caught salmon fillet, sliced into 8 portions
- 50g green onions, chopped
- 2.3g paprika
- 2.8g soy sauce powder
- 1.7g salt

Serving: 4

Calories: 401

Protein: 40g

Carbs: 6g

Fat: 7g

Fibre: 1.2g

Directions:

1. Combine all the ingredients in a large bowl and stir until well blended. Set aside.
2. Preheat your air fryer to its highest temperature. Place the salmon filets into the air fryer and cook for 4 minutes.
3. Using a spatula, gently flip and cook for a further 4 minutes or until cooked through. Set aside.

Aged Macadamia Nut Salmon

Total time: 16 minutes

Preparation time: 6 minutes

Cooking time: 10 minutes

Ingredients required:

- 227g salmon fillet, skin intact
- 5ml olive oil
- 75ml macadamia nuts
- 15ml lemon juice
- 2.5ml honey

For Sauce

- 15ml butter
- 30ml honey
- 185ml soy sauce (kenji or shoyu)
- 1 pinch freshly ground pepper

Serving: 2

Calories: 478

Protein: 16.6g

Carbs: 9.8g

Fat: 35.6g

Fibre: 1.7g

Directions:

1. For sauce, add all the ingredients in a small bowl and mix until well combined.
2. Heat up the air fryer to 175 degrees Celsius (347 degrees Fahrenheit) and set the timer to 10 minutes.
3. Wash the salmon fillet and pat dry with a towel.
4. Coat the salmon fillet with olive oil, lemon juice and honey using your hands. Rub the mixture until completely absorbed. Sprinkle over some freshly ground pepper for seasoning.
5. Once the salmon has cooked; transfer to a plate and allow to rest for 10 minutes.
6. Add the sauce to the air fryer and mix well, cook until it thickens. Dish up and serve immediately.
7. Divide into two servings with some fresh vegetables of your choice.

Air Fryer Fish Stir-Fry

Total time: 25 minutes

Preparation time: 10 minutes

Cooking time: 15 minutes

Ingredients required:

- 85g macadamia nuts, roughly chopped
- 100g fresh salmon fillet, skin intact
- 105g asparagus, sliced into 1 inch.
- 1.5g lime juice
- 1.5g lime zest
- 2g salt
- 0.7g pepper

Serving: 2

Calories: 441

Protein: 24.5g

Carbs: 18.3g

Fat: 26.5g

Fibre: 5.8g

Directions:

1. Add all the ingredients in a large bowl and mix until well combined, set aside.
2. Once the asparagus is cooked; transfer to a plate and allow to rest for 5 minutes.
3. Divide into two servings with some fresh vegetables of your choice (over brown rice).

Air Fryer Fish Tacos

Total time: 25 minutes

Preparation time: 10 minutes

Cooking time: 15 minutes

Ingredients required:

- 100g salmon fillet, skin intact
- 40g mango salsa (store-bought or home-made)
- 1g salt

Serving: 2

Calories: 261

Protein: 25.1g

Carbs: 14.2g

Fat: 10.4g

Fibre: 5.1g

Directions:

1. Add all ingredients in a large bowl and mix until well combined, set aside.
2. Divide into two servings with some fresh vegetables of your choice.
3. Enjoy immediately after cooking.

Dill Crust Roast Salmon with Thyme & Butter Sauce

Total time: 25 minutes

Preparation time: 10 minutes

Cooking time: 15 minutes

Ingredients required:

- 600g salmon fillet, cut in half lengthwise and skin on (.600)
- 90g frozen mixed vegetables (sweetcorn, carrots, onions and peas)
- 30ml vegetable stock (no added salt)
- 15g dried dill leaves
- 2.5g salt
- 4.5g cracked black pepper

Serving: 2

Calories: 202

Protein: 29.5g

Carbs: 7.1g

Fat: 10.9g

Fibre: 2.3g

Directions:

1. Preheat your air fryer to its highest temperature. Place the salmon halves in the air fryer and cook for 5 minutes. After 5 minutes has elapsed, flip, brush with butter and cook until cooked through and golden brown.
2. While the salmon is cooking, combine the vegetable stock and dried dill in a saucepan on the stovetop, bring to a boil and pour over the roasted salmon.
3. Transfer to a serving plate and serve with mashed potatoes or asparagus.

Air Fryer Teriyaki Salmon Fillets with Broccoli

Total time: 45 minutes

Preparation time: 15 minutes

Cooking time: 30 minutes

Ingredients required:

- 4 x 150g salmon fillets
- 60ml teriyaki sauce
- 60g brown sugar
- 15ml rice vinegar
- 250g broccoli, cut into florets

Serving: 4

Calories: 354

Protein: 29g

Carbs: 35g

Fat: 11g

Fibre: 4.5g

Directions:

1. Season the salmon with salt and pepper then set aside. Whisk together teriyaki sauce and brown sugar until smooth. Add a splash of water if it is too thick. Set aside.

2. In a large bowl, combine broccoli florets with rice vinegar and set aside.

3. In your air fryer, add salmon fillets and broccoli, pour over the teriyaki sauce mixture and cook at 170C for 15 minutes.

CHAPTER 6: VEGETERIAN RECIPES

Air Fryer Poached Pears

Total time: 25 minutes

Preparation time: 5 minutes

Cooking time: 20 minutes

Ingredients required:

- 4 x 90g pears, peeled
- 60ml orange juice
- 30ml coconut water
- 2.5g cinnamon powder
- 2g nutmeg powder

Serving: 4

Calories: 301

Protein: 3.2g

Carbs: 46g

Fat: 0g

Fibre: 1.9g

Directions:

1. Half fill your air fryer with water and place a plate on top of the water.
2. This creates a steam chamber. Place the pears on top of the plate and set aside.
3. In the bowl of your air fryer, add orange juice, coconut water and spices. Stir well to combine.

Air Fryer Cauliflower

Total time: 20minutes

Preparation time: 5 minutes

Cooking time: 15 minutes

Ingredients required:

- 500g cauliflower
- 250ml water
- 50ml milk
- 30ml oil
- 1 onion
- 20g butter
- 2g black pepper
- 1.5g salt

Serving: 4

Calories: 390

Protein: 8g

Carbs: 38g

Fat: 5.6g

Fibre: 6.7g

Directions:

1. Cut the cauliflower into florets. Mix the water and milk together and add to a large container with the cauliflower in it. Microwave for 10 minutes on full power.
2. Drain the cauliflower thoroughly and pat dry with kitchen paper.
3. Toss with the oil, pepper and salt. Set to Air Fry for 10 minutes at 250°F (121°C).
4. Add the butter and onion. Stir until combined before serving.

Air Fryer Courgette

Total time: 20minutes

Preparation time: 5 minutes

Cooking time: 15 minutes

Ingredients required:

- 800g courgette
- 200g mushrooms (button)
- 20ml olive oil
- 1 onion
- 1.5g salt

Serving: 4

Calories: 271

Protein: 4g

Carbs: 35g

Fat: 2.8g

Fibre: 6.9g

Directions:

1. Wash and slice the courgette into half inch thick rounds.
2. Add the olive oil, if desired. Set to Air Fry for 15 minutes at 250°F (121°C).
3. Add the mushrooms, onion and salt and cook for 3-4 minutes.
4. Stir the mushroom mixture before serving.

Air Fryer Kidney Beans

Total time: 20minutes

Preparation time: 5 minutes

Cooking time: 15 minutes

Ingredients required:

- 200g kidney beans (pintos)
- 5g garlic
- 20ml olive oil
- 1 onion
- 1.5g salt
- 75ml water

Serving: 4
Calories: 459
Protein: 26.8g
Carbs: 30g
Fat: 16.9g
Fibre: 20.6g

Directions:

1. Wash and cover the kidney beans with boiling water to soften them.
2. Set aside for 10 minutes to cool. Drain thoroughly.
3. Cut the pinto beans into halves and toss with salt, pepper and oil before setting to Air Fry for 10 minutes at 250°F (121°C).
4. Add the onion and garlic. Stir until combined before serving.

Air Fryer Mushrooms

Total time: 20minutes

Preparation time: 5 minutes

Cooking time: 15 minutes

Ingredients required:

- 450g mushrooms, sliced
- 35ml olive oil (use more if needed)
- 25g butter
- 5ml dried parsley, plus extra for garnish
- 1.5g black pepper
- 1.5g salt
- 1.5g cayenne pepper
- 2.5g paprika
- 2g garlic powder
- 2.5g oregano, dried and finely chopped
- 1.5g cumin seed (plus extra for sprinkling)

Serving: 4

Calories: 180

Protein: 3.6g

Carbs: 5.5g

Fat: 13g

Fibre: 2.1g

Directions:

1. Place salt, pepper and garlic powder in the air fryer-safe bowl then set aside.
2. In your air fryer, cook mushrooms at 170C for 8 minutes or until cooked through. Set aside.
3. Place butter in the air fryer-safe bowl, melt at 170C for 1 minute or until golden brown. Set aside with butter to cool slightly.
4. After 8 minutes, add in paprika and cayenne pepper to the air fryer-safe bowl then mix well until combined. Set aside.
5. In your air fryer, drizzle in some oil and set the temperature to 180C.
6. Place mushroom mixture on baking tray, drizzle over some oil and add in parsley.
7. Place mushrooms on the higher rack, drizzle butter mixture and cook for further 5 minutes or until golden brown in colour. Set aside with butter to cool slightly.
8. To serve, divide mushrooms between two plates then drizzle over some sauce and sprinkle with oregano and cumin powder. Serve with a side salad or toasted brown rice or quinoa.

Air Fryer Aubergine Parmesan

Total time: 15 minutes

Preparation time: 5 minutes

Cooking time: 10 minutes

Ingredients required:

- 800g aubergine
- 60ml water
- 10g garlic
- 1 onion
- 3g salt
- 6g parmesan cheese
- 5g olive oil

Serving: 4 (makes 10 slices)

Calories: 234

Protein: 7.5g

Carbs: 19.5g

Fat: 15.2g

Fibre: 12.8g

Directions:

1. Cut the aubergine lengthwise and skin them.
2. Slice the aubergine into halves and then into half inch thick slices.
3. Set the Air Fryer to 250°F (121°C) for 10 minutes.
4. Toss the slices with salt, pepper, oil and water if desired.
5. Toss them again before adding the remaining ingredients.
6. Place in a serving plate, if desired, and serve while hot.

Potato and Kale Croquettes

Total time: 18 minutes

Preparation time: 9 minutes

Cooking time: 9 minutes

Ingredients required:

- 4 eggs, slightly beaten
- 42g flour
- 42g cup goat cheese, crumbled
- 8.5g fine sea salt
- 4 garlic cloves, minced
- 125g kale, steamed
- 41.6g cup breadcrumbs
- 1.8g red pepper flakes
- 3 potatoes, peeled and quartered
- 1.8g teaspoon dried dill weed

Serving: 4

Calories: 660

Protein: 17.6g

Carbs: 58.4g

Fat: 39.9g

Fibre: 12.5g

Directions:

1. Firstly, boil the potatoes in salted water. Once the potatoes are cooked, mash them; add the kale, goat cheese, minced garlic, sea salt, red pepper flakes, dill, and one egg; stir to combine well.

2. Now, roll the mixture to form small croquettes.

3. Grab three shallow bowls. Place the flour in the first shallow bowl.

4. Beat the remaining 3 eggs in the second bowl. After that, throw the breadcrumbs into the third shallow bowl.

5. Dip each croquette in the flour; then, dip them in the eggs bowl; lastly, roll each croquette in the breadcrumbs.

6. Air fry at 335 degrees F for 7 minutes or until golden. Tate, adjust for seasonings, and serve warm

Air Fryer Avocado Rolls with Spicy Salmon and Wasabi Dip

Total time: 22 minutes

Preparation time: 5 minutes

Cooking time: 27 minutes

Ingredients required:

- 200g salmon fillet, sliced into 8 portions
- 160ml wasabi paste
- 160ml water
- 2 x 100g avocados, sliced into 4 portions (replace with cucumbers)
- 0.9g salt, to taste
- 2g pepper
- 1.7g paprika powder
- 2.7g garlic, crushed
- 1.5g white onion powder

Serving: 4

Calories: 309

Protein: 19g

Carbs: 31g

Fat: 19g

Fibre: 7.5g

Directions:

1. In a bowl, mix all spices together and season with the spice mixture. Set aside.
2. Add water to the bowl of your air fryer and place a plate on top to create a steam chamber.
3. Drop the salmon fillets into the basket and cook for 12 minutes at 170C under Low to Medium fan speed.
4. In a small bowl, whisk wasabi paste with water until well combined then transfer to the air fryer basket with the salmon. Cook for 7 minutes at 170C under Low fan speed.
5. Add avocado slices and cook for 3 minutes under Low to Medium fan speed. When done, remove air fryer basket and set aside on a plate until ready to serve. Serve immediately with the fresh wasabi dip.

Air Fryer Broccoli (Turnip)

Total time: 15 minutes

Preparation time: 5 minutes

Cooking time: 10 minutes

Ingredients required:

- 800g broccoli, stems and florets
- 100g parmesan cheese, seasoned to taste
- 20g butter
- 5g garlic
- 1.5g salt
- 2g parmesan cheese, seasoned to taste

Serving: 4

Calories: 247

Protein: 12.3g

Carbs: 23g

Fat: 5.8g

Fibre: 16.7g

Directions:

1. Wash the broccoli thoroughly. Dry it in a salad spinner, if desired.
2. Microwave for 10 minutes on full power and drain thoroughly.
3. Combine the ingredients for flavouring in a serving plate and set aside before adding the broccoli.
4. Set to Air Fry for 3 minutes at 250°F (121°C).
5. While gliding the chips around you can gently toss them so they don't burn.
6. Toss again before serving.

Air Fryer Tater Tots

Total time: 25 minutes

Preparation time: 5 minutes

Cooking time: 20 minutes

Ingredients required:

- 400g sweet potato or yam, (peeled and diced)
- 50ml water
- 5g garlic
- 2g salt
- 2.2g bacon bits
- 1 onion

Serving: 4

Calories: 360

Protein: 3g

Carbs: 51.9g

Fat: 9.8g

Fibre: 4.3g

Directions:

1. Cook the sweet potato on full power. Drain the sweet potato thoroughly, if desired.
2. Cut the potato into small cubes and place in a serving plate.
3. Microwave for 20 minutes on full power or until the potato cubes are soft and cooked through. Stir occasionally. Mash the potato and add salt, pepper and bacon bits if desired.
4. Set to Air Fry for 10 minutes at 250°F (121°C).
5. While gliding the sweet potato around you can gently toss it. Toss before serving.

Air Fryer Potatoes

Total time: 25 minutes

Preparation time: 5 minutes

Cooking time:20 minutes

Ingredients required:

- 400g potatoes (yukon gold or waxy)
- 20g butter
- 1 onion
- 2g salt
- 50ml water

Serving: 4

Calories: 437

Protein: 3.2g

Carbs: 100g

Fat: 27.1g

Fibre: 14.2g

Directions:

1. Wash the potato properly. Cut into fries and toss with salt and butter.
2. Set the Air Fryer to 250°F (121°C) for 15 minutes.
3. Add onion, if desired and cook for 5 more minutes.

CHAPTER 7: APPETIZER RECIPES

Double Cheese Mushroom Balls

Total time: 45 minutes

Preparation time: 15 minutes

Cooking time: 30 minutes

Ingredients required:

- 45ml olive oil
- 112g cauliflower florets
- 3 garlic cloves, peeled and minced
- 1/2 yellow onion, finely chopped
- 62.5g roasted vegetable stock
- 250g white mushrooms, finely chopped
- Sea salt and ground black pepper, or more to taste
- 62.5g Swiss cheese, grated
- 31g pork rinds
- 1 egg, beaten
- 31g Romano cheese, grated
- 1 small-sized red chili pepper, seeded and minced

Serving: 4

Calories: 176

Protein: 5.3g

Carbs: 2.9g

Fat: 16.4g

Fibre: 1g

Directions:

1. Blitz the cauliflower florets in your food processor until they're crumbled (it is the size of rice).

2. Heat a saucepan over moderate heat; now, heat the oil and sweat the cauliflower. Garlic, onions, and chili pepper until tender.

3. Throw in the mushrooms and fry until they are fragrant and the liquid almost evaporates.

4. Add the vegetable stock and boil for 18 minutes. Add salt, black pepper, Swiss cheese pork rinds, and beaten egg; mix to combine.

5. Allow the mixture to cool completely. Shape the mixture into balls. Dip the balls in the grated Romano cheese. Air-fry the balls for 7 minutes at 400 degrees F. Bon appétit!

Air Fryer Lemon Pepper Wings

Total time: 50 minutes

Preparation time: 10 minutes

Cooking time: 40 minutes

Ingredients required:

- 2.5kg chicken wings
- 30ml olive oil
- 30ml lemon juice
- 400 ml buttermilk
- 30ml white vinegar
- 7g salt
- 7g garlic powder
- 7g onion powder

Serving: 4

Calories: 130

Protein: 12.5g

Carbs: 9g

Fat: 6g

Fibre: 0.5g

Directions:

1. Coat the chicken wings in buttermilk and transfer to a large mixing bowl. Add salt, garlic powder, onion powder and lemon juice to the chicken wings and mix well.
2. Add white vinegar to a large rectangular roasting pan.
3. Arrange the chicken wings on the wire rack. Pour the chicken wings and buttermilk into the roasting pan and transfer to a preheated 350F oven.
4. Bake at 35-40 minutes, or until the chicken wings are no longer pink in the centre. Remove from the oven and allow to cool.
5. In a small bowl, mix all sauce ingredients together until smooth. Pour the sauce over the chicken wings and toss until evenly coated in sauce.
6. Serve with celery sticks, blue cheese dressing or ranch dressing on the side for dipping!

Air Fryer Croutons

Total time: 35 minutes

Preparation time: 10 minutes

Cooking time: 25 minutes

Ingredients required:

- 3g salt
- 1.3g pepper
- 2g sesame seeds, toasted and roughly chopped
- 2g garlic, toasted and roughly minced
- 2g parmesan cheese, grated

Serving: 4

Calories: 165

Protein: 5g

Carbs: 11g

Fat: 12g

Fibre: 2.5g

Directions:

1. Place salt, pepper and sesame seeds in the air fryer-safe bowl and mix well until combined. Set aside.
2. Add garlic to the air fryer-safe bowl and mix well. Add parmesan cheese and stir until combined. Add croutons to the bowl and stir until well coated with cheese mixture. Set aside.
3. Spread croutons evenly on a baking tray and cook at 180C for 15 minutes or until golden brown in colour.
4. Allow to cool before serving. Store in an airtight container for up to 4 days in the fridge.

Sesame Air Fryer Cashews

Total time: 40 minutes

Preparation time: 10 minutes

Cooking time: 30 minutes

Ingredients required:

- 250g cashew nuts
- 2g salt
- 1.2g garlic powder
- 1.2g onion powder
- 2g sesame seeds, toasted and roughly chopped

Serving: 4	
Calories: 174	
Protein: 6g	
Carbs: 12g	
Fat: 15g	
Fibre: 4g	

Directions:

1. Place cashews on an oven tray lined with baking paper. Transfer to a preheated 180C oven and bake for 15 minutes or until golden brown in colour.
2. Remove from the oven and set aside. Add salt, garlic powder, onion powder and sesame seeds to the air fryer-safe bowl. Mix well until combined.
3. Add cashews to the air fryer basket and carefully toss until the cashews are evenly coated in spice mixture. Transfer the cashews to an oven tray lined with baking paper.
4. Bake at 180C for 15 minutes or until crispy. Remove and set aside to cool before serving. Store in an airtight container for up to 4 days in the fridge.

Air Fryer Cheese Curds

Total time: 1 hour

Preparation time: 20 minutes

Cooking time: 40 minutes

Ingredients required:

- 450g mozzarella cheese, cut into 1 inch cubes
- 15ml white vinegar
- 30ml milk
- 30ml vegetable oil
- 30ml parmesan cheese, grated

Serving: 4

Calories: 220

Protein: 21.5g

Carbs: 0g

Fat: 18g

Fibre: 0g

Directions:

1. In a small bowl, mix milk and white vinegar together. Stir to combine well.
2. Add the cubed mozzarella cheese to a medium mixing bowl and pour in the milk/white vinegar/oil mixture over top of it.
3. Add grated parmesan cheese, salt and pepper to the mozzarella and stir to combine.
4. Tie up a piece of parchment paper over the cheese and twist the ends tight.
5. Pour the cheese in a deep fryer basket lined with paper towels, if you don't have one, use aluminum foil instead.
6. Put your deep fryer on 350F and lower in the bowl of cheese so that it's completely submerged in oil when it's hot enough (about 2 minutes).
7. Fry for about 10 minutes, or until the cheese becomes bubbly and starts floating to the top.
8. Remove from the fryer basket, twist and serve warm!

Air Fryer Marsala Spinach

Total time: 55 minutes

Preparation time: 5 minutes

Cooking time: 50 minutes

Ingredients required:

- 25g butter, softened (can use coconut oil instead)
- 200g marsala wine
- 500g fresh spinach leaves

Serving: 4

Calories: 100

Protein: 4g

Carbs: 0g

Fat: 7g

Fibre: 0g

Directions:

1. In a small bowl, mix the butter (or coconut oil) and marsala wine together until well combined.
2. Heat the deep fryer on 375F and lower in the basket of spinach so that it's submerged in oil when it's hot enough (about 5 minutes).
3. Cook for about 15 minutes, or until the spinach is wilted.
4. Remove from the oil and transfer to a clean paper towel.
5. In a small microwave safe bowl, mix the marsala mixture with half of the spinach and microwave for 2 minutes (or until heated through).
6. Repeat with the remaining spinach and marsala mixture, until all of the spinach is wilted and heated through.
7. Serve warm with a side of lemon wedges, and maybe some roasted garlic.

Beetroot Risotto With Cashews And Mushrooms

Total time: 30 minutes

Preparation time: 10 minutes

Cooking time: 20 minutes

Ingredients required:

- 1 large beetroot, peeled and diced
- 2 garlic cloves, minced
- 30ml olive oil
- 10ml lemon juice
- 1kg mushrooms (button), sliced
- 1 medium onion, finely chopped
- 3g salt
- 3g pepper ground
- 1.5g lovely spice mix (add more if desired)

Serving: 4

Calories: 181

Protein: 9g

Carbs: 7g

Fat: 12g

Fibre: 0.5g

Directions:

1. Add salt and pepper to the air fryer-safe bowl. Mix well until combined. Set aside.
2. Spread the diced beetroot on a baking tray lined with baking paper. Transfer to an air fryer and cook at 180C for 10 minutes or until the beetroot is cooked through.
3. Combine all ingredients, except for the air fryer-safe bowl, in a large pot and bring to a boil. Reduce heat to medium-low and simmer for 15 minutes or until the liquid has reduced by half.
4. Transfer to an air fryer-safe bowl* and serve immediately. Store any leftover risotto in an airtight container in the refrigerator for up to 4 days.
5. If you are cooking for 2 or more people, it is recommended to use the larger air fryer-safe bowl.

Total time: 45 minutes

Preparation time: 20 minutes

Cooking time: 25 minutes

Ingredients required:

- 2.5kg pork belly, cut into 1 inch cubes
- 30ml coconut oil
- 1 garlic bulb, chopped
- 14g salt
- 14g pepper
- 4 large sweet potatoes (about 1kg), peeled and cut into 1 inch cubes.

Serving: 4

Calories: 340

Protein: 25g

Carbs: 15g

Fat: 23g

Fibre: 1g

Directions:

1. Coat the sweet potatoes in coconut oil and add to a large mixing bowl. Add salt and pepper to the bowl as well. Add garlic cloves to the bowl and mix well.
2. In a large rectangular roasting pan, arrange the pork belly cubes on the wire rack. Add the bowl of sweet potatoes and garlic to the pan.
3. Transfer to a preheated 350F oven and bake for 10 minutes. Flip all ingredients over so that they are evenly baked and transfer to a preheated 375F oven and bake for 15 minutes more, or until all of the sweet potatoes are tender when pierced with a fork (pork belly should be crispy on top).
4. Remove from the oven and allow to cool on the wire rack. Once cool, transfer to a large mixing bowl and add the sauce mixture.
5. Toss to coat all of the sweet potatoes in sauce. Serve warm or at room temperature with your favourite side dishes!

Air Fryer Cold Appetizers

Total time: 40 minutes

Preparation time: 10 minutes

Cooking time: 30 minutes

Ingredients required:

- 100g carrots, cut into 0.5cm sticks
- 100g red onions, sliced into rings
- 3.5ml vinegar
- 30ml vegetable oil
- 1tbsp honey

Serving: 8

Calories: 110

Protein: 0.5g

Carbs: 17g

Fat: 7g

Fibre: 3.5g

Directions:

1. In a deep fryer basket, combine all ingredients and heat until oil is hot (about 2 minutes).
2. Cook at 350F for 10 minutes.
3. Turn off deep fryer and allow to cool.
4. Transfer to a large mixing bowl and add the sauce mixture.
5. Toss to coat all of the onions and carrots in sauce.
6. Serve at room temperature with your favourite side dishes.

Air Fryer Baked Mushrooms

Total time: 50 minutes

Preparation time: 10 minutes

Cooking time: 40 minutes

Ingredients required:

- 1200g button mushrooms
- 3tbsp butter, melted
- 125g swiss cheese, grated
- 3tbsp Parmesan cheese, grated
- 50ml heavy cream

Serving: 4

Calories: 110

Protein: 0.5g

Carbs: 12g

Fat: 7g

Fibre: 3g

Directions:

1. Preheat the oven to 375F.
2. In a small mixing bowl, mix together all ingredients (including heavy cream).
3. Spread the cheese/mushroom mixture evenly on a baking sheet.
4. Bake for 20 minutes at 375F.
5. Remove from the oven and allow to cool on the wire rack.
6. Once cool, transfer to a large mixing bowl and add the sauce mixture.
7. Toss to coat all of the mushrooms in sauce.
8. Serve at room temperature with your favourite side dishes.

Air Fryer Garlic Sauce

Total time: 10 minutes

Preparation time: 2 minutes

Cooking time: 8 minutes

Ingredients required:

- 4 medium garlic cloves, minced
- 10ml oil (can use butter instead)
- 30ml water (or more if you like a watery sauce)
- 5ml vinegar

Serving: 1

Calories: 40

Protein: 0.5g

Carbs: 0g

Fat:3g

Fibre: 0g

Directions:

1. Heat the deep fryer to 375F and lower in the basket of garlic so that it's completely submerged in oil when it's hot enough (about 2 minutes).
2. Cook until browned, about 1 minute.
3. Remove from the fryer basket and place the garlic on a paper towel to drain excess oil.
4. Set aside for about a minute and transfer it to a small mixing bowl.
5. Add the oil, water, and vinegar to the bowl with garlic and mix until well combined.
6. Serve warm!

CHAPTER 8: DESSERT RECIPES

Air Fryer Pumpkin Pie

Total time: 55 minutes

Preparation time: 10 minutes

Cooking time: 45 minutes

Ingredients required:

- 450g pumpkin
- 80g cream cheese
- 54g egg yolks
- 8ml vanilla extract
- 175ml milk (I used skim)
- 40g caster sugar
- 180g cream cheese

Serving: 6

Calories: 291

Protein: 13g

Carbs: 50g

Fat: 18g

Fibre: 6g

Directions:

1. Preheat your oven to 160C. Add the pumpkin, egg yolks, 4.5ml vanilla extract and milk to a food processor and puree until smooth.
2. Pour the pureed mixture into a round cake pan (approx 8 inches) lined with parchment paper in your air fryer and cook at 170C for 15 minutes.
3. Remove from the air fryer, add the rest of the vanilla extract and cream cheese to the mixture and mix well. Increase your oven temperature to 180C and cook for another 20 minutes until golden brown on top.

Air Fryer fruit pudding

Total time: 35 minutes

Preparation time: 10 minutes

Cooking time: 25 minutes

Ingredients required:

For topping:

- ½ tsp baking powder
- 2 tbsp milk
- 1 egg
- 2 tbsp sugar
- 56g soft butter
- 84g flour

For filling:

- 125g fresh or canned sliced fruit

Serving: 4

Calories: 250

Protein: 5g

Carbs: 48g

Fat: 15g

Fibre: 2g

Directions:

1. Air fryer should be preheated to 320 degrees Fahrenheit or 160 degrees Celsius.
2. In a separate dish, combine the ingredients for the "topping." After a thorough beating for three minutes, the mixture should be smooth and creamy.
3. Put the ingredients for the "filling" in a baking dish, then pour the topping mixture on top of the fruit and spread it out evenly.
4. Bake in an air fryer that has been prepared to 320 degrees Fahrenheit or 160 degrees Celsius for 25 to 30 minutes, or till golden brown.

Air Fryer Banana Bread

Total time: 35 minutes

Preparation time: 10 minutes

Cooking time: 25 minutes

Ingredients required:

For topping:

- 150g all-purpose flour
- 5ml ground cinnamon
- 40g light brown sugar
- 2.5mls vanilla extract
- 80g unsalted butter
- 180ml whole milk
- 3 large eggs (beaten)
- 4 overripe bananas

Serving: 6

Calories: 315

Protein: 10g

Carbs: 44g

Fat: 14g

Fibre: 3.6g

Directions:

1. In a medium bowl, whisk together the flour, cinnamon, brown sugar and salt. Add the butter and mix until it resembles coarse crumbs.
2. Whisk together the milk, eggs and vanilla extract in a separate bowl until pale yellow in colour then pour into the flour/butter mixture and mix until just combined with no large lumps of flour remaining.
3. Line a tray with parchment paper and spread half of the batter on top. Mix the bananas for 10 seconds in your food processor then spread on top of batter. Cover with the remaining batter and repeat steps 2-4.
4. Transfer to your air fryer and cook at 160C for 12-15 minutes or until golden brown and cooked through after removing from the oven.

Air Fryer Special Brownies

Total time: 35 minutes

Preparation time: 10 minutes

Cooking time: 25 minutes

Ingredients required:

- 200g caster sugar
- 5g baking powder
- 1.5mls vanilla extract
- 175ml whole milk
- 2 large eggs (beaten)
- 100g unsalted butter, melted
- 250g dark chocolate, melted (I used 100% cocoa solids)
- 150g plain flour

Serving: 6

Calories: 577

Protein: 10g

Carbs: 69g

Fat: 38g

Fibre: 7g

Directions:

1. In a medium bowl, whisk together the flour, caster sugar and baking powder; set aside.
2. Whisk together the eggs, milk, vanilla extract and melted butter in another bowl until the batter is pale yellow in colour.
3. Pour into the flour mixture and mix until just combined with no large lumps of flour remaining.
4. Line a tray with parchment paper; pour half of the batter on top. Drizzle with half of the melted chocolate, followed by the other half of the batter then drizzle with the rest of the melted chocolate.
5. Transfer to your air fryer and cook at 170C for 15 minutes or until cooked through after removing from the oven. Cut into 16 even pieces.

Air Fryer Strawberry Cobbler

Total time: 40 minutes

Preparation time: 15 minutes

Cooking time: 25 minutes

Ingredients required:

Serving: 6

Calories: 199

Protein: 2.5g

Carbs: 27g

Fat: 8.5g

Fibre: 4.8g

- 170g old fashioned oats
- 180g whole milk
- 10ml orange oil (I used sweet orange)
- 50g honey
- 145g unsalted butter, melted and slightly cooled.
- 1 egg (beaten)
- 300g fresh strawberries, washed and seeded.
- 1 orange (for zest)

Directions:

1. Line a tray with parchment paper.
2. In a bowl, combine the oats, 120g of melted butter, orange oil, and honey; mix until combined.
3. Pour the mixture onto the tray and spread evenly. Place another sheet of parchment paper on top then roll out until even and about 1/4-inch thick. Remove top parchment paper then transfer to your air fryer.
4. Cook at 170C for 15 minutes or until golden brown and cooked through after removing from the oven. Allow to cool completely then cut into 9 pieces.

Air Fryer Tasty Orange Biscuits

Total time: 50 minutes

Preparation time: 10 minutes

Cooking time: 40 minutes

Ingredients required:

- 140g unsalted butter, melted and slightly cooled
- 140g dark brown sugar
- 2.5mls vanilla extract
- 1 medium egg (beaten)
- 80g self raising flour
- 2.5mls orange oil (I used sweet orange)
- 75g golden syrup
- 275g oranges, peeled and segmented then zested.

Serving: 6

Calories: 297

Protein: 1g

Carbs: 46g

Fat: 12g

Fibre: 4.5g

Directions:

1. In a mixing bowl, combine the melted butter, brown sugar and vanilla extract then beat until it's smooth and creamy in texture.
2. Whisk in the egg and combine well then add the flour, orange oil and golden syrup followed by the orange zest and mix until just combined with no large lumps of flour remaining.
3. Line a baking tray with parchment paper then spoon half of the mixture onto the tray and spread out evenly to form a thin layer (no thicker than 5mm) then repeat steps 2-3 then transfer to your air fryer.
4. Bake at 170C for 15 minutes or until cooked through after removing from the oven.
5. Increase your oven temperature to 200C and cook for another 10 minutes until golden brown on top.

Air Fryer Egg Tarts

Total time: 19 minutes

Preparation time: 10 minutes

Cooking time: 9 minutes

Serving: 4
Calories: 282
Protein: 4.2g
Carbs: 44.3g
Fat: 8g
Fibre: 0.8g

Ingredients required:

- 4 frozen egg custard tarts

Directions:

1. Remove packaging of frozen egg custard tarts keeping the foil container.
2. Place the foiled egg custard in the air fryer.
3. Ensure that the egg custard tarts are separate from each other. They should not be at top of one another.
4. At 160 degrees Celsius or 320 Fahrenheit, air fryer the tarts before serving.
5. Remove packaging of frozen egg custard tarts keeping the foil container.
6. Place the foiled egg custard in the air fryer.
7. Ensure that the egg custard tarts are separate from each other. They should not be at top of one another.
8. At 160 degrees Celsius or 320 Fahrenheit, air fryer the tarts before serving.

Air Fryer Apple Fries

Total time: 20 minutes

Preparation time: 5 minutes

Cooking time: 15 minutes

Ingredients required:

- 6 apples of medium size
- 1 tbsp cinnamon
- 32ml extra virgin avocado oil

Serving: 4-5
Calories: 178
Protein: 1g
Carbs: 39g
Fat: 1.2g
Fibre: 8g

Directions:

1. Thinly slice the medium sized apples using mandolin or some other thing similar to it.
2. Toss the sliced apples in extra virgin avocado oil or preferred healthy oil.
3. Sprinkle the apples in cinnamon.
4. Place the sliced apples in air fryer at temperature of 200 degrees Celsius or 400 degrees Fahrenheit and cook them for 15 minutes.
5. Serve apple fries with seasoning of your choice.

Air Fryer banana chips

Total time: 3 hours 5 minutes

Preparation time: 5 minutes

Cooking time: 3 hours

Ingredients required:

- 3 large bananas
- 2 tbsp Stevia
- Extra virgin oil for spraying

| Serving: 4-5 |
| Calories: 77 |
| Protein: 1g |
| Carbs: 20g |
| Fat: 1g |
| Fibre: 2g |

Directions:

1. Peel the bananas and slice them to the same level of thickness.
2. Add lemon juice to the bowl, add bananas to it and gently toss. Ensure that you do not break banana slices.
3. Remove the banana slices using a spoon.
4. Place banana slices on air fryer's tray. They should be placed separately and must not be at top of each other.
5. Spray the slices with extra virgin oil and sprinkle them with Stevia.
6. Place them in the air fryer at 55 degrees Celsius or 130 degrees Fahrenheit for three hours.
7. Allow them to cool and store them in containers for later use.

CHAPTER 9: STARTER RECIPES

Air Fryer Potato Chips

Total time: 29 minutes

Preparation time: 20 minutes

Cooking time: 9 minutes

Ingredients required:

- 160 g French fries, cut into wedges (or other crisps/chips)
- 1 medium egg white
- 125 ml milk
- 5g all-purpose flour, sifted
- 0.3g baking powder
- 60ml canola

Serving: 8

Calories: 92

Protein: 3.2g

Carbs: 15g

Fat: 3.3g

Fibre: 1g

Directions:

1. Preheat the air fryer to 200C/400F/Gas mark 6. Place a wire rack over a large plate and place the potato wedges on top then transfer them onto the rack.
2. Brush the potatoes with oil, then coat with eggs white, milk, flour and baking powder (once combined), in that order.
3. Cook for 9 minutes at 200C/400F/Gas mark 6, turn them once halfway through cooking time to ensure even browning.
4. Once cooked, transfer the chips to a bowl and season to taste with salt.

Air Fryer Crab Cakes

Total time: 30 minutes

Preparation time: 20 minutes

Cooking time: 10 minutes

Ingredients required:

- 380g crab meat, picked
- 60ml canola oil, divided
- 15g fresh breadcrumbs
- 20g onion, chopped finely
- 1 large egg, lightly beaten
- 31g mayonnaise
- 1 medium clove garlic, crushed or minced
- 1g ground sweet paprika
- 1g salt

Serving: 4
Calories: 281
Protein: 20g
Carbs: 7g
Fat: 18g
Fibre: 0.5g

Directions:

1. Blend the crab meat, canola oil, egg and mayonnaise in a large bowl then stir in the onion and garlic.
2. Pour the mixture into a food processor or blender and purée to form a smooth batter. If a blender is used, chill the mixture in an ice bath before processing.
3. Transfer the batter to a large bowl then fold in the breadcrumbs, paprika and salt until evenly blended together then shape into patties with your hands.
4. Cook the crab cakes over a medium heat outside of the air fryer for 10 minutes at 200C/400F/Gas mark 6, turning once halfway through cooking time.

Air Fryer French Fries

Total time: 28 minutes

Preparation time: 20 minutes

Cooking time: 8 minutes

Ingredients required:

- 50g cornflour
- 0.1g salt
- 240g potatoes, peeled and cut into wedges
- 1.4g pepper

Serving: 6

Calories: 88

Protein: 1g

Carbs: 17g

Fat: 0.2g

Fibre: 3.5g

Directions:

1. Place the potatoes into a medium-sized bowl, then sprinkle with cornflour, salt and pepper. Press down on the potatoes once more to ensure that the cornflour is evenly distributed.
2. Preheat the air fryer to 200C/400F/Gas mark 6, add a wire rack to the basket then place the wedges onto it (make sure they aren't touching each other).
3. Cook for 8 minutes at 200C/400F/Gas mark 6, then transfer to a tray or plate and serve immediately.

Air Fryer Pigs In A Blanket

Total time: 28 minutes

Preparation time: 20 minutes

Cooking time: 8 minutes

Ingredients required:

- 550g sausage meat
- 40g parsley, chopped finely
- 15g onion, chopped finely
- 1.5g garlic, crushed or minced
- 3g oregano
- 2g paprika powder (preferably smoked)
- 1.3g salt

Serving:4

Calories: 35

Protein: 2g

Carbs: 1g

Fat: 1.2g

Fibre: 2.5g

Directions:

1. Combine all the ingredients in a bowl then mix well until thoroughly blended together.
2. Shape the sausage mixture into 8 sausages with your hands, then place each one onto a square of cling film, roll it up and seal both ends to form a sausage shape.
3. Cook each sausage for 10 minutes at 200C/400F/Gas mark 6, turning once halfway through cooking time to ensure even browning.

Air Fryer Carrot Fries

Total time: 28 minutes

Preparation time: 20 minutes

Cooking time: 8 minutes

Ingredients required:

- 160g potatoes, cut into wedges
- 25g fresh breadcrumbs
- 3g salt
- 0.4g freshly ground pepper
- 1g garlic powder
- 1.5g onion powder
- 1g paprika powder

Serving:4

Calories: 112

Protein: 2.5g

Carbs: 22g

Fat: 14g

Fibre: 2.3g

Directions:

1. Place the potatoes into a medium-sized bowl, then sprinkle with breadcrumbs, salt and pepper. Press down on the potatoes once more to ensure that the breadcrumbs are evenly distributed.
2. Preheat the air fryer to 200C/400F/Gas mark 6, add a wire rack to the basket then place the wedges onto it (make sure they aren't touching each other).
3. Cook for 8 minutes at 200C/400F/Gas mark 6, then transfer to a tray or plate and serve immediately.

Air Fryer Cheese Crackers

Total time: 25 minutes

Preparation time: 15 minutes

Cooking time: 10 minutes

Ingredients required:

- 120g polenta, ground finely
- 0.1g salt
- 50ml water
- 1.5g paprika powder
- 30ml canola oil, plus extra for brushing

Serving: 8	
Calories: 90	
Protein: 3g	
Carbs: 18g	
Fat: 1.7g	
Fibre:1.7g	

Directions:

1. Combine the polenta and salt in a medium bowl then add the water and mix well until thoroughly blended together.
2. Transfer the mixture onto a clean work surface and work it into a ball, pressing down on it with the palm of your hand to form a flat disk of dough.
3. Preheat the air fryer to 200C/400F/Gas mark 6, place a wire rack over a large plate and transfer the dough onto it then brush with canola oil and season with paprika (once combined) then transfer to the basket.
4. Cook for 10 minutes at 200C/400F/Gas mark 6, then transfer to a wire rack to cool before serving.

Air Fryer Chickpeas

Total time: 20 minutes

Preparation time: 5 minutes

Cooking time: 15 minutes

Ingredients required:

- 539g can of chickpeas (drained and rinsed)
- 15ml olive oil
- 1g salt
- 0.4g garlic powder
- 0.6g onion powder
- 1.2g paprika
- 0.5g cayenne (optional)

Serving: 4

Calories: 165

Protein: 8g

Carbs: 16g

Fat: 1g

Fibre:5.5g

Directions:

1 .Heat air fryer to 390°F / 200°C.

2. Drain and rinse chickpeas (no need to dry). Toss with olive oil and spices.

3. Dump the whole batch of chickpeas in the air fryer basket. Cook for 12-15 minutes, shaking a couple of times.

4. When chickpeas are cooked to your liking, remove from air fryer, taste and add more salt and pepper to taste.

5. Store in an open container.

Air Fryer Salad Bites

Total time: 34 minutes

Preparation time: 20 minutes

Cooking time: 14 minutes

Ingredients required:

- 50g tin chickpeas (drained and rinsed)
- 1g garlic powder
- 0.3g onion powder
- 0.3g paprika
- 1.7g poppy seeds
- 1.5g salt

Serving: 4

Calories: 165

Protein: 7g

Carbs: 20g

Fat: 1g

Fibre:4.5g

Directions:

1. Preheat the air fryer to 390°F / 200°C, add a wire rack to the basket then place all the salad ingredients into it (except for the salt) then transfer them onto it.
2. Cook for 14 minutes at 390°F / 200°C, then add the salt and cook for another 2-3 minutes at 390°F / 200°C.
3. Remove from the basket and serve immediately.

Air Fryer Sweetcorn Fritters

Total time: 27 minutes

Preparation time: 15minutes

Cooking time: 12 minutes

Ingredients required:

- 55g plain flour
- 50g sunflower seeds, ground finely
- 50g finely grated parmesan cheese
- 2.5g salt (or to taste)
- 1.3g cayenne (optional)
- 1.3g paprika

Serving: 4

Calories: 118

Protein: 4g

Carbs: 16g

Fat: 2g

Fibre: 3.7g

Directions:

1. Preheat the air fryer to 390°F / 200°C, place a wire rack over a large plate then transfer the sweetcorn and flour into a medium-sized bowl and toss them together.
2. Transfer the sweetcorn and flour mixture onto a clean work surface, press down on it with your hands to form a flat disk of dough then press down on it again with the palm of your hand to flatten it further.
3. Combine the sunflower seeds and parmesan in a medium-sized glass bowl then mix in the salt, cayenne and paprika. Divide the mixture into 8 equal portions and make into balls, then flatten each ball into a disc using the palm of your hand to have a consistent thickness throughout.
4. Place each disc on a plate or tray and cook for 8 minutes at 390°F / 200°C, turning once halfway through cooking time to ensure even browning.
5. Serve immediately.

Air Fryer Avocado Filled Squares

Total time: 25 minutes

Preparation time: 15minutes

Cooking time: 10 minutes

Ingredients required:

- 60g mixed seeds, including flaxseeds, hemp and chia
- 1 small avocado, peeled and pitted
- 20g sunflower seeds, ground finely
- 1.3g salt (or to taste)
- 1.7g paprika

Serving: 4

Calories: 128

Protein: 7g

Carbs: 14g

Fat: 3.2g

Fibre: 2g

Directions:

1. Preheat the air fryer to 390°F / 200°C, place a wire rack over a large plate then transfer the mixed seeds and avocados into a medium-sized bowl and toss them together.
2. Transfer the mixed seeds and avocados onto a clean work surface, press down on it with your hands to form a flat disk of dough then press down on it again with the palm of your hand to flatten it further.
3. Combine the sunflower seeds and paprika in a medium-sized glass bowl then mix in the salt.
4. Divide the mixture into 4 equal portions and make into balls, then flatten each ball into a disc using the palm of your hand to have a consistent thickness throughout.
5. Place each disc on a plate or tray and cook for 6-10 minutes at 390°F / 200°C, turning once halfway through cooking time to ensure even browning. Serve immediately with avocado dipping sauce.

14-Days Meal Plan

	Breakfast	Lunch	Dinner	Desserts
Day 1	Herb-roasted Cauliflower, pg11	Easy Air Fryer Rice With Mushrooms And Caramelized Onions, pg22	Air Fryer Pork Chops, pg46	Air Fryer Pumpkin Pie, pg93
Day 2	Air Fryer Bacon And Eggs, pg11	Air Fryer Fish Fillets with Chive Butter, pg58	Air Fryer Macaroni and Cheese, pg24	Air Fryer fruit pudding, pg94
Day 3	Air Fryer Chicken Courgette Fritters, pg12	Air Fryer Lunch Pork and Potatoes, pg26	Tarragon And Spring Onions Salmon, pg61	Air Fryer Banana Bread, pg95
Day 4	Yummy Brownies, pg14	Prawns Scampi with Spicy Pepper Sauce, pg57	Air Fryer Bacon-Wrapped Hot Dogs, pg47	Air Fryer Special Brownies, pg96
Day 5	Air Fryer Scrambled Eggs, pg15	Air Fryer Teriyaki Salmon Fillets with Broccoli, pg59	Air Fryer Juicy Steak Bites, pg48	Air Fryer Strawberry Cobbler, pg97
Day 6	Air Fryer Sausage Biscuits, pg16	Air Fryer Cauliflower, pg70	Air Fryer Meat Loaf, pg49	Air Fryer Egg Tarts , pg99
Day 7	Air Fryer Pancakes With Blueberries, pg18	Air Fryer Avocado Rolls with Spicy Salmon and Wasabi Dip, pg76	Air Fryer Salmon Teriyaki, pg62	Air Fryer Tasty Orange Biscuits, pg98
Day 8	Egg Salad with Asparagus and Spinach, pg17	Air Fryer Courgette, pg71	Air Fryer Bacon Cheeseburgers, pg50	Air Fryer Apple Fries, pg100
Day 9	Air Fryer Cinnamon Pancakes, pg19	Air Fryer Mushrooms, pg73	Air Fryer Ribeye Steak, pg53	Air Fryer banana chips, pg101

Day 10	Easy Cheesy Broccoli, pg20	Air Fryer Tater Tots, pg78	Prawns with Lemon and Pepper Sauce, pg56	Air Fryer Potato Chips, pg103
Day 11	Air Fryer Sweetcorn Fritters, pg111	Air Fryer Aubergine Parmesan, pg74	Air Fryer Garlic Butter Steaks, pg54	Air Fryer Pigs In A Blanket, pg106
Day 12	Air Fryer Cheese Curds, pg85	Dill Crust Roast Salmon with Thyme & Butter Sauce, pg66	Air Fryer Kidney Beans, pg72	Air Fryer Carrot Fries, pg107
Day 13	Air Fryer Pigs In A Blanket, pg106	Air Fryer Potatoes, pg79	Air Fryer Baked Mushrooms, pg90	Air Fryer Chickpeas, pg109
Day 14	Air Fryer Avocado Filled Squares, pg112	Tuna with Roasted Garlic and Hazelnuts, pg60	Air Fryer Garlic Sauce, pg91	Herb-roasted Cauliflower, pg11

CONCLUSION

Thank you and congratulation for using this cookbook to learn how to prepare delicious and healthy recipes in an Air Fryer. I hope you found these recipes helpful and tasty. Now that we are at the end of this cookbook, I wanted to share one last tip with you. It's a tip I learned from my grandma when she was making desserts.

First, she would melt chocolate or caramel in a small saucepan over medium heat.

Once it was melted, she would add enough sugar to create the desired consistency and stir it until all the granules of sugar have dissolved in the mixture. The result is a delicious, smooth, and creamy chocolate or caramel that you can top any dessert. Enjoy!

Printed in Great Britain
by Amazon